WOMEN, WORK AND WAGES

GILDA BERGER

WOMEN, WORK AND WAGES

FRANKLIN WATTS 1986
NEW YORK LONDON TORONTO SYDNEY

Charts and graphs by Vantage Art.

Photographs courtesy of: UPI/Bettmann Newsphotos: pp. 6, 7, 35, 75, 109; Punch/Rothco Cartoons: pp. 28, 96; Rothco Cartoons: p. 51; Archives of Labor and Urban Affairs/Wayne State University: p. 72; Smith College Archives/Smith College: p. 84.

Library of Congress Cataloging in Publication Data

Berger, Gilda.
Women, work, and wages.

Bibliography: p.
Includes index.
Summary: Examines women in the work force in the United States, with an emphasis on sex discrimination and related problems.
1. Women—Employment—United States. 2. Equal pay for equal work—United States.   4. Sexual harassment of women—United States. [1. Women—Employment. 2. Sex discrimination against women] I. Title.
HD6095.B47   1986   331.4'0973   85-15379
ISBN 0-531-10074-X

CONTENTS

I

A GROWING
PART
OF THE
WORK FORCE

THE FACTS

In 1960 there were approximately 23 million working women. They made up more than 30 percent of the nation's work force. Today there are nearly 50 million women holding jobs, which is about 45 percent of all workers.

Over the past twenty years the number of employed men increased by about 27 percent. But the number of employed women rose at three times that rate.

Currently, more than two of every three adult women under thirty work, compared with two of every five in 1960.

Fifty-five percent of all mothers who have children under the age of eighteen are in the labor force.

Since 1960 the number of two-earner families has risen by 3 million to 29.5 million. This represents 60 percent of all married-couple families.

More than 13.5 million women entered the labor force in the decade from 1972 to 1981, compared with fewer than 8 million men joining the labor force during that same period.

Two of every three entrants to the labor market in the late 1980s and 1990s are expected to be women. And it is forecast that women will fill seven of every ten new jobs created during this period.

Nine of every ten girls today will work in paid employment for 25 to 45 years. As heads of households, two of five women will be responsible for the support of children and others.

Ida graduated from high school at eighteen and was married one year later. Between graduation and the birth of her first child, Ida worked as a stock clerk in a department store at $8,500 a year. Her husband was working for a large auto maker, earning an annual wage of about $25,000. They bought a house and a new car. After the baby was born, Ida decided she wanted to stay home and care for the child.

Soon after their second child was born, Ida's husband was laid off. Ida had to go back to work. The store rehired her at the same wage as when she had first started. The couple lived on her salary and his unemployment benefits while he looked for a job. But they had to borrow money to make their mortgage and car payments and keep up with their other expenses. When her husband finally got a job, it was as a plumber's helper earning $20,000 annually. Now, with the two incomes, Ida and her family are able to make ends meet.

In many ways Ida is typical of the large numbers of women who now work outside the home and earn wages for the work they do. According to the latest statistics, an estimated 75 percent of women work because they need to support themselves and/or their families. For most women—married, divorced, or single—working is a necessity.

Married women living with out-of-work husbands are usually the sole source of family income. Married women living with low-earning spouses, too, must work to put bread on the table. But even when the husband earns a decent living, today's economy makes it difficult for most families to get along on only one paycheck. As economists George Sternlieb and James W. Hughes said in a recent study: "The good life in America increasingly requires a household economic team of two workers."

As a result, we find today that nearly three-fifths of all married couples in the United States have two incomes. That is many more than in the past. Employed wives who work full-time outside the home contribute more than 40 percent of the average family's income.

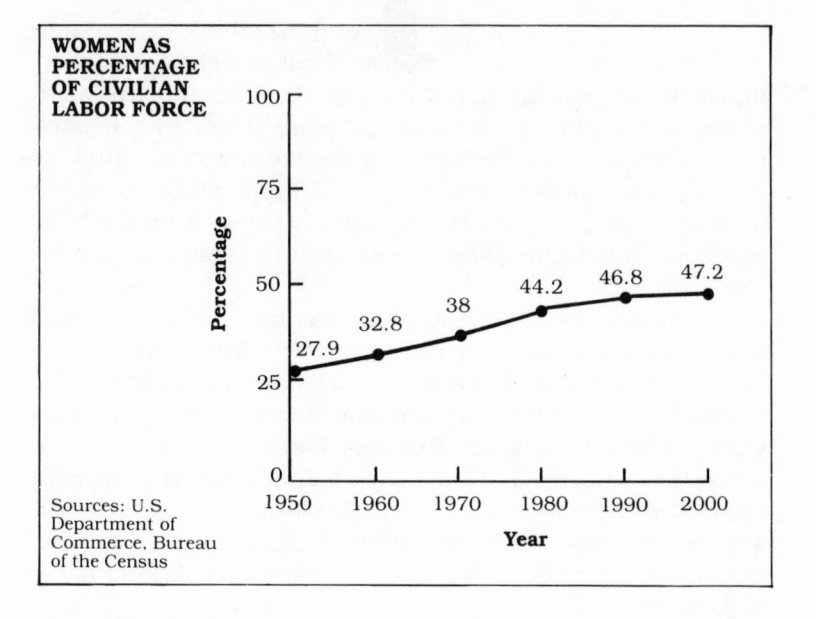

WOMEN AS PERCENTAGE OF CIVILIAN LABOR FORCE

Percentage

27.9 32.8 38 44.2 46.8 47.2

1950 1960 1970 1980 1990 2000

Year

Sources: U.S. Department of Commerce, Bureau of the Census

The high rate of divorce (about 50 percent of all marriages) has significantly affected the economic status of many women, too. A California study of three thousand divorced couples found that one year after divorce the wife's income dropped by 73 percent.

Many more women are now remaining single than ever before. Without the economic support of a man, these women must work outside the home. They have no other source of income.

As society has been changing, more and more women are becoming the source of income for a growing proportion of families in the United States. About 25 percent of all families were supported by a woman in 1981, compared with only 21 percent in 1975.

Right now only 25 percent of American families fit the traditional pattern of a father who works and a mother who stays home with the children. This trend is terribly important. It affects not only the work place but the basic structure of society as well.

WHERE ARE
WOMEN WORKING?

Today there are women at work in more industries and professions than ever before. Many women are now becoming anything they want to be—bankers, ministers, rabbis, accountants, miners, firefighters, police officers, bartenders. The road signs no longer say Men at Work. Today many read People at Work, because women are also involved in road building and construction. One woman has been appointed to the Supreme Court and another was nominated to be vice-president of the United States. Nearly 14 percent of the nation's lawyers are female. So are nearly 15 percent of its doctors and 39 percent of its computer programmers and systems analysts.

The facts show that many of the barriers are coming down for women seeking employment. Current legislation makes it illegal to discriminate against women in hiring, training, promotion, and other employment practices. In addition, many laws forbidding discriminatory practices are helping women. Affirmative action, for example, requires employers to take steps to treat women as the equals of men in hiring. Other government programs and policies help women gain entry to training, education, and employment openings that were previously denied them. As a result, women now work in just about every job category.

But the situation is far from ideal. The facts show that women are still not equal to men in the wages they earn or the jobs they hold. Various kinds of discrimination and prejudice place women at a disadvantage in the labor force.

Women, for instance, still face only a limited range of employment choices. More than half the women are employed in just 20 of the 421 types of jobs listed in the Department of Labor's *Dictionary of Occupational Titles.* In 1982 more than one-half of all employed women worked in occupations that are 75 percent female; 22 percent of employed women worked in occupations that are more than 95 percent female. And the work traditionally done by women is usually paid less and valued less than the so-called men's jobs.

Facing page: The Democratic party's vice presidential candidate during the 1984 presidential campaign was Geraldine Ferraro, shown here with her mother, Antonetta Ferraro, after returning to New York from the convention in San Francisco. *Above:* Sandra Day O'Connor was appointed to the U.S. Supreme Court in 1981.

The greatest number of women in the work force (about 28 million, roughly 66 percent of all employed women) hold white-collar jobs—clerical, sales, professional, technical, administrative, and managerial. Although such jobs are very important to society, many are not well paid or highly regarded.

About 6 million women (14 percent of all working women) are in blue-collar jobs, as craft workers, machine operators, or nonfarm laborers. Most women in this group (78 percent) work as machine operators in factories, another low-paid, undervalued area.

Approximately 20 percent of all employed women (8 million) are service workers. They work in private households or in health, food, personal, and protective services. Women far outnumber men in this occupational group, accounting for about 62 percent of all service workers. This group earns among the lowest wages of all. They are also often the least appreciated.

Finally, fewer than 2 percent of all working women are employed on the farm as farmers, managers, laborers, and supervisors. They account for only 18 percent of all farm workers.

The concentration of women into a few occupations is one reason that women, on the average, earn only about 60 percent of what men earn. Women are more apt to work as tellers at banks than as bank officers, to sell cosmetics than cars, to teach in elementary school than in college, to use a computer than to program it.

Most women working in business are employed in or near entry-level jobs, such as clerks or assistants, for example. Entry-level jobs are, of course, paid the lowest wages.

This clustering of women at the lower end of the job scale probably has several causes. It may be because many more women have recently entered the work force. Or it may be due to the fact that numbers of women return to work after child rearing. But even after taking these factors into consideration, experts say it is most likely due to discrimination. This discrimination is usually based on the underestimation of women's skills, education, and experience.

To be sure, some women are now entering occupations traditionally dominated by men. From 1962 to 1982 the proportion of women engineers rose from 1 to 4 percent. Among mail carriers the increase was from 3 to 17 percent; butchers 4 to 16 percent; physicians 6 to almost 15 percent; insurance agents 10 to 24 percent; bartenders 11 to nearly 50 percent; bus drivers 12 to 47 percent; and college teachers 19 to 35 percent. But even these women who are working in fields not usually occupied by women are often earning less than men doing the same work.

A very small number of women are working in such fast-growing occupations as computer programmers, mathematicians, systems analysts, and industrial engineers. These women have been able to narrow the gap between their wages and the wages received by men. But the actual number of women engaged in these occupations remains relatively small. The majority of women in new high-tech industries are still grouped in modern versions of clerical and service-oriented jobs. And they receive the same low pay.

Women also now work in insurance, once a high-paid field dominated by men. The insurance industry today hires many women to do dull, repetitive work that is largely done at computer terminals. Women now hold 65 percent of these low-paying jobs, up 27 percent from 1970.

Under the present system, too, few women are reaching the top in their fields. In the automated, high-technology electronics industry, the top managers are highly trained, well paid, and mostly male. The bulk of the staff is production workers, with limited skills and low wages, and they are, for the most part, female.

Catalyst, a New York based research group, says that only about eight of every one thousand employed women hold high-level executive, administrative, or managerial jobs. Women occupy only 3 percent of the sixteen thousand seats on the boards of the thousand largest corporations listed by *Fortune* magazine. While 80 percent of the members of the garment workers' union are women, only two of the twenty-six executive board members are. Based on their membership, "women get half the number of leadership positions

EMPLOYED PERSONS IN SELECTED OCCUPATIONS, BY SEX, ANNUAL AVERAGES, 1981

Occupation	Women			Men	
	Number (in thousands)	Percent distribution	As percent of total employment	Number (in thousands)	Percent distribution
Total	**43,000**	**100.0**	**42.8**	**57,397**	**100.0**
White-Collar Workers	**28,328**	**65.9**	**53.5**	**24,621**	**42.9**
Professional and technical workers	7,319	17.0	44.6	9,100	15.9
Accountants	434	1.0	38.5	692	1.2
Computer specialists	170	0.4	27.1	458	0.8
Librarians, archivists, curators	159	0.4	82.8	33	0.1
Personnel and labor relations workers	220	0.5	49.9	221	0.4
Physicians	62	0.1	13.7	392	0.7
Registered nurses	1,296	3.0	96.8	44	0.1
Health technologists and technicians	465	1.1	72.3	178	0.3
Social workers	249	0.6	63.8	141	0.2
Teachers, college and university	206	0.5	35.2	380	0.7
Teachers (except college and university)	2,257	5.2	70.6	940	1.6
Elementary school teachers	1,180	2.7	83.6	232	0.4
Kindergarten and prekindergarten teachers	241	0.6	98.4	4	(¹)
Secondary school teachers	632	1.5	51.3	599	1.0
Engineering and science technicians	214	0.5	18.8	927	1.6
Writers, artists, and entertainers	553	1.3	39.8	834	1.5
Managers and administrators (except farm)	3,168	7.4	27.5	8,372	14.6

Occupation					
Bank officers and financial managers	261	0.6	37.5	435	0.8
Buyers and purchasing agents	167	0.4	35.1	309	0.5
Restaurant, cafeteria, and bar managers	293	0.7	40.3	434	0.8
Sales managers and department heads (retail trade)	139	0.3	40.2	206	0.4
School administrators	156	0.4	36.3	274	0.5
Sales workers	2,916	6.8	45.4	3,509	6.1
Hucksters and peddlers	135	0.3	79.4	35	0.1
Insurance agents, brokers, and underwriters	142	0.3	23.9	453	0.8
Real estate agents and brokers	280	0.7	49.8	282	0.5
Sales clerks (retail trade)	1,730	4.0	71.2	702	1.2
Clerical workers	14,938	34.7	80.5	3,626	6.3
Bank tellers	532	1.2	93.5	37	0.1
Billing clerks	135	0.3	88.2	18	[1]
Bookkeepers	1,786	4.2	91.1	175	0.3
Cashiers	1,431	3.3	86.2	229	0.4
Counter clerks (except food)	275	0.6	76.4	85	0.1
Estimators and investigators (n.e.c.)	295	0.7	54.6	245	0.4
File clerks	264	0.6	83.8	51	0.1
Computer and peripheral equipment operators	360	0.8	63.8	204	0.4
Keypunch operators	232	0.5	93.5	15	[1]
Payroll and timekeeping clerks	187	0.4	81.0	44	0.1
Postal clerks	102	0.2	37.9	167	0.3
Receptionists	657	1.5	97.3	17	[1]
Secretaries	3,883	9.0	99.1	34	0.1
Shipping and receiving clerks	118	0.3	22.5	406	0.7
Statistical clerks	297	0.7	80.3	73	0.1
Stock clerks and storekeepers	184	0.4	34.8	344	0.6
Teachers aides (except school monitors)	354	0.8	92.9	27	[1]
Telephone operators	286	0.7	92.9	22	[1]
Typists	993	2.3	96.3	38	0.1

EMPLOYED PERSONS IN SELECTED OCCUPATIONS, BY SEX, ANNUAL AVERAGES, 1981

Occupation	Women			Men	
	Number (in thousands)	Percent distribution	As percent of total employment	Number (in thousands)	Percent distribution
Total	**43,000**	**100.0**	**42.8**	**57,397**	**100.0**
Blue-Collar Workers	**5,815**	**13.5**	**18.6**	**25,446**	**44.3**
Craft and kindred workers	802	1.9	6.3	11,859	20.7
Blue-collar supervisors	205	0.5	11.3	1,611	2.8
Printing craft workers	100	0.2	24.9	302	0.5
Operatives (including transport)	4,499	10.5	32.1	9,517	16.6
Assemblers	611	1.4	52.4	556	1.0
Checkers, examiners and inspectors (manufacturing)	430	1.0	53.8	369	0.6
Clothes ironers and pressers	95	0.2	80.5	23	(¹)
Dressmakers and seamstresses (except factory)	114	0.3	97.4	3	(¹)
Laundry and dry cleaning operators (n.e.c.)	129	0.3	66.5	66	0.1
Packers and wrappers	372	0.9	63.2	217	0.4
Sewers and stitchers	775	1.8	96.0	32	0.1
Textile operatives	183	0.4	61.0	116	0.2
Bus drivers	170	0.4	47.2	190	0.3
Nonfarm laborers	527	1.2	11.5	4,056	7.1
Stockhandlers	244	0.6	24.6	749	1.3

	8,342	19.4	62.1	5,097	8.9
Service Workers					
Private household workers	1,010	2.3	96.5	38	1.0
Child care workers	440	1.0	97.6	11	[1]
Private household cleaners and servants	445	1.0	95.1	22	[1]
Service workers (except private household)	7,332	17.1	59.2	5,059	8.8
Cleaning service workers	961	2.2	38.6	1,528	2.7
Building interior cleaners	528	1.2	55.3	427	0.7
Lodging quarters cleaners	175	0.4	97.2	5	[1]
Janitors and sextons	258	0.6	19.1	1,096	1.9
Food service workers	3,101	7.2	66.2	1,581	2.8
Bartenders	149	0.3	47.3	166	0.3
Cooks	723	1.7	51.9	670	1.2
Dishwashers	73	0.2	28.5	183	0.3
Food counter and fountain workers	391	0.9	83.7	77	0.1
Waiters, waitresses, and helpers	1,363	3.1	89.2	338	0.6
Health service workers	1,780	4.1	80.1	215	0.4
Dental assistants	139	0.3	97.2	4	[1]
Health aides and trainees (excluding nursing)	261	0.6	84.2	48	0.1
Nursing aides, orderlies, and attendants	979	2.3	86.6	152	0.3
Practical nurses	394	0.9	97.8	10	[1]
Personal service workers	1,342	3.1	76.0	424	0.7
Child care workers	407	0.9	95.5	19	[1]
Hairdressers and cosmetologists	515	1.2	89.3	62	0.1
Farm Workers	**489**	**1.1**	**17.8**	**2,260**	**3.9**
Farmers and farm managers	168	0.4	11.3	1,317	2.3
Farm laborers and supervisors	322	0.7	25.5	943	1.6
Farm laborers (wage workers)	154	0.4	15.9	815	1.4
Farm laborers (unpaid family workers)	165	0.4	65.0	89	0.2

[1] Number too small for reliable estimate.

Source: *Employment and Earnings*, March 1982, U.S. Department of Labor, Bureau of Labor Statistics.

EMPLOYMENT STATUS OF WOMEN IN POVERTY
WHO MAINTAIN FAMILIES, BY RACE, 1981 [1]
(Numbers in thousands)

	All races	
Employment status	Below poverty level	Percent of total
Total	3,252	34.6
In civilian labor force	1,286	22.6
Employed	926	18.3
Unemployed	360	57.7
Not in civilian labor force	1,966	53.0

[1] Persons 15 years of age and over.

they're entitled to in most unions," says Anne H. Nelson, associate director of Cornell University's Institute for Education and Research on Women and Work.

WHY THE FEMINIZATION
OF POVERTY?

The Census Bureau has said that poverty is increasingly becoming a woman's problem. The term *feminization of poverty* refers to the fact that women make up the majority of the poor. Right now two of every three adults at or below the poverty level are women.

Women's poverty is due in part to the male-female wage gap. Of women who work full-time throughout the year, 32 percent earn only $10,000 or less (compared with less than 13 percent of men working full-time). Further, a good deal of the increase in poverty in the last decade can be explained by the increase in numbers of households headed by women. Of those households 40 percent are at or below the poverty level.

White		Black	
Below poverty level	**Percent of total**	**Below poverty level**	**Percent of total**
1,814	27.4	1,377	52.9
745	18.1	520	35.7
572	15.2	334	28.2
173	49.7	186	69.1
1,069	42.8	856	74.6

Source: U.S. Department of Commerce, Bureau of the Census.

More evidence of the feminization of poverty comes from statistics on the way government aid to the poor is divided. Ninety-three percent of Aid to Families with Dependent Children goes to women and children, and at least 85 percent of food stamp recipients are women and children.

More than 40 percent of single-parent families, almost all women heads of households, fail to receive court-ordered support from the absent parent. Of those that do, only 47 percent actually receive the full amount of this essential benefit. "Sixty to eighty percent of the children eligible for child support receive none," according to the Women's Legal Defense Fund.

The Child Support Enforcement Act was passed on August 16, 1984. This new law helps women to collect unpaid child support payments from the fathers of their children. It requires states to begin withholding child support from the paycheck of any parent who can be shown to be more than thirty days behind in child support payments. The state then gives the money to the parent who has custody of the child.

Although child support payments are generally not the primary source of income for people who receive them, the 1981 poverty rate (17 percent) for women getting such payments was considerably lower than the rate for women who did not get them (41 percent). In many instances women near the poverty line who received child support would fall below this level if those payments were to stop.

Aging women, especially if divorced or widowed, are often forced to live in poverty. In 1983 the median income for women over sixty-five was $5,600, which is barely above the official poverty level. Older women tend to be poorer and have less income than men of the same age. Even taking into account the fact that there are more older women than men, an unusually high percentage of the elderly poor (about 75 percent) are women.

Many among the elderly women had held jobs but left them to raise their children. Those who returned to work often had to begin again with entry-level jobs and salaries. Many lost pensions and other benefits because their service in the work force was interrupted. A good number of these women did not even get survivor's benefits because their former or late husbands had pension plans that did not pay divorced wives or widows. And finally, most lost out throughout their lives by low salaries and lack of employment opportunities.

WHO IS RESPONSIBLE?

The disadvantages of women in the work world result from many factors. Very important are employers' outdated ideas of "women's work" and outright discrimination. Many employers choose to keep unfairness from dying out. They do little or nothing to change situations that treat women unjustly.

Women are much more likely to be employed in jobs that are part-time, temporary, or seasonal. They are also among the last to be hired. Therefore, when jobs are scarce and there are layoffs, they are among the first to be fired.

Unemployment tends to impact on women more than men. The unemployment rate for women auto workers (30 percent in 1982), for example, is much higher than for men doing the same work (18 percent). In the female-dominated garment industry the unemployment rate has been as much as 60 percent above the national average.

In 1982 single women maintaining families with children under eighteen suffered from 17.3 percent unemployment, while the overall unemployment rate was only 10.9 percent. The rate two years later was 11 percent, which was still higher than the average for either men or women.

In addition to unemployment there is another related problem for women in the work place—underemployment. Because of either discrimination in the labor market or heavy home and child care responsibilities, many women are forced to settle for low-paying jobs with fewer benefits, for part-time work, or for jobs that offer little or no overtime.

There have been some advances in training women to do "nontraditional" kinds of work. But women still find it hard to get into programs that train workers for skilled jobs as construction workers, plumbers, carpenters, and so on. Such training is essential if women are to move into more of the blue-collar jobs not usually held by women. What is needed is more programs designed to improve the position of women as skilled workers.

A lack of child care facilities is also responsible for holding back large numbers of working women. Many mothers, eager and able to work, are unable to do so because they have no one to care for their very young children. Still others cannot afford the high cost of child care. Without affordable child care, women get locked into the low-paying jobs. Jobs on this level carry little responsibility and enable women to take time off to care for their children when necessary. These jobs also provide little opportunity to move up to higher-salaried positions.

Annoying behavior on the part of employers and other workers, ranging from poking fun to physical abuse, plague many women on the job. This behavior, called sexual harassment, affects both how well women do their jobs and how likely they are to advance. As more employers take steps to end harassment, women will be able to enter more fields not usually occupied by women and work more successfully with male managers and co-workers.

The number of occupations that traditionally employ women is growing. But at the same time many of these jobs are being lost through automation. Some women are being displaced by machines, such as automated bank tellers, advanced office equipment, and industrial robots. A study by Wassily Leontif and Faye Duchin of New York University reports that computers in the office dramatically improve productivity. At the same time, though, they lead to a "steep decline in the relative number of clerical workers."

In the past there were large offices filled with rows of clerks, supervised by a staff of managers and assistant managers. In today's automated work places the women often sit alone in tiny cubicles. In front of each woman is a computer terminal into which she systematically enters numbers and other data. There is no need for a supervisor; the computer itself monitors her rate of production. If the worker falls below her hourly work quota, it sets off an automatic signal.

Because there are fewer supervisors in automated industries, there are fewer opportunities for women to move up to higher salaries. The effect, some fear, is that women will remain on the lowest clerical level forever.

Someday automation may actually help to solve some of the problems of working wives and mothers. Women employees may not have to go to the office at all. The machines will be installed in their homes and be connected electronically to the central office. This will free women to work at home on a flexible schedule, solving child care and many other problems.

One danger, though, is that automation may also lead to a piecework pay system. Under this system the worker is paid for the units of work completed, not for the time it takes. The result of piecework pay is usually low pay and no benefits. This is the situation that now seems to be developing in the electronics industry in California.

Officials at Nine to Five, an organization which helps women office workers organize into unions, are concerned about the rise of office automation and employers' preference for part-time workers paid on a piecework basis. The organization is afraid that automation will lead to low wages, no security, and no health insurance, pensions, or other benefits. "Automation is producing the sweatshops of the eighties," said Janice Blood, former director of public information for Nine to Five.

According to a study on the effect of office automation published by *Working Woman*, women office workers will not really benefit from automated equipment as it is currently being introduced. "The first step towards the 'office of the future,' " the study states, "is to apply the principle of factory production to office work." One company executive said, "Business can finally monitor and measure clerical function."

WHAT CAN BE DONE?

For a long while individuals and groups have been trying to find ways to improve women's position in the work place. Until recently these remedies have been made up mainly of efforts to encourage and enable women to move into the so-called men's jobs—firefighters, carpenters, pilots, astronauts, and so on. But now there are new approaches to solving inequality in the work place. One of the main ways is to take a new look at, and upgrade the value of, so-called women's jobs. As women's jobs become more comparable to men's jobs, the wages paid women will improve.

More women, it is also expected, will join labor unions. Women union members (less than 12 percent of today's labor force) generally enjoy higher wages, better benefits, and superior working conditions compared with those of nonunion workers. As they become organized, women workers seek to improve conditions even more. But they still have far to go. A Maryland postal worker was recently elected the first female officer of her union local. When she showed up at the union office on the first day, though, the local's president said, "Oh, I'm so glad they elected you vice-president. Now we can finally get the files straightened out."

Also, automation can work to women's advantage. Those who enroll in the right courses in school will be able to make gains in the electronic, automated world of tomorrow. Women who study subjects like mathematics and engineering will probably find jobs in technology, where knowledge and ability count. Those who become experts in the field of computers and the management and processing of information will likely succeed in finding more interesting, better-paying jobs.

Dr. Winifred Warnat, director of the National Center on Teaching and Learning, refers to computer-literate people as "the information haves." These "haves" will be able to adapt to the new technology and make decisions on how automation is to be used. The "have nots" will be unable to cope with the changes brought on by automation. Information and skill are valuable keys that can open doors to good jobs for millions of working women.

Strong enforcement of existing laws and new legal action would help women in their fight for better employment opportunities and more nearly equal pay. But laws alone cannot change employers' perception of the working woman. For women to be treated as men's equals on the job they need to be seen as individuals—individuals who need and want to work.

The number of working women of all ages—married, single, divorced, widowed—has more than tripled since the period immediately preceding World War II (1940). Fewer children per family and a planned spacing between children have made more mothers available to join the work force. A longer life expectancy also has allowed more women to take jobs. The desire for an improved sense of self-worth and a more varied life role has brought more women into the work place. And a slowly changing acceptance of women as workers has contributed to women's increased participation in the labor market.

According to the Department of Labor, over the next ten years two-thirds of the growth in the labor force will be accounted for by women. An improvement in working women's opportunities and working conditions can only benefit everyone—men, women, and children.

II

EQUAL PAY

THE FACTS

The median wage for full-time women workers in the United States is $13,000; for full-time men workers it is $21,077—an earnings gap of 40 percent. Put another way, women earn only 60 cents for every dollar paid to men; it takes women nine days to earn what men earn in five.

Among people who work for the government, the wage difference is especially striking. Women make $15,579 on an average, while men earn an average of $30,553.

The pay gap is as wide today as decades ago, but there are signs that it is getting narrower. At the present rate of improvement, it is estimated that by 1995 women still will earn only 74 cents to every dollar earned by men.

Thirty-two percent of all female workers are now paid less than $10,000 a year, while only 13 percent of men fall into this category.

At the upper end of the scale, 5 percent of all women make more then $25,000 per year, while more than 33 percent of all men earn that amount.

Female college graduates earn an average of $16,322 per year. This amount is only slightly above that of men with only an eighth-grade education.

A full 80 percent of all women in the work force are found in the twenty lowest-paying occupations.

Alice is a secretary in a New York sales office. She got her job two years ago when she was eighteen years old. Since then she has worked hard but has received no increase in salary, no training opportunities, and no promotion. Her typewriter is old and slow, with keys that stick, and she works in a small, poorly ventilated room where the copying machine is also located.

From time to time Alice has talked to her employer about her frustrations in using the old typewriter and her fears about working so near the fumes from the copying machine, a potential health hazard. But each time he told her that she was "hired help" and that she should do her best with what she had to work with. He also implied that her experience did not count for very much and that she was not too valuable to the firm.

Once or twice Alice has talked over her problems on the job with the other secretaries in the same office. She even asked them to join her in speaking up for themselves. Most did not seem interested or concerned. Others said they were afraid of losing their jobs.

Recently Alice heard about a group of clerical workers, all of them women, who had formed a New York chapter of Nine to Five, the National Association for Working Women. Alice joined and got two other secretaries to become members as well. Now when she speaks to her boss, he listens to what she has to say. He has already given her a better typewriter and promised to move the copying machine out of her office.

Of the 48 million women in the labor force, about 75 percent are clustered in the so-called pink ghetto. These are the "women's jobs"—clericals, salespeople, private household workers, waitresses, hairdressers, and other low-level positions. Even those women who work in professional and technical positions do different work from men. Over half are concentrated in teaching, social work, and health careers. This situation, in which men and women are grouped by sex into different occupations, is called occupational segregation.

Even within a certain occupation, industry, or firm, women and men may do different jobs. This is known as job segregation. As just one example of job segregation, women who teach at colleges or universities are more likely to be professors of English; men are more likely to be professors of engineering.

The fact that men and women do different work in our country has helped create the wage gap between men and women. Other factors contribute as well. About one of every four women works in a female-dominated and usually low-paid position. To take just a few examples: Women are 99 percent of all secretaries (average annual salary, $12,000), 97 percent of all dressmakers and seamstresses ($8,200), and 94 percent of all bank tellers ($9,800).

Women are seldom found in jobs with the highest pay and the greatest opportunity for advancement. They make up only 5.8 percent of all engineers and 1.4 percent of all carpenters, both traditionally high-paying fields. The bituminous coal industry, for example, ranks first in average earnings. It is fifty-second in percentage of women employees. On the other hand, the apparel and textile industry ranks first in female employment. It is fiftieth in average hourly earnings.

Even where women work in high-paying industries, women's earnings are almost always lower than men's. Barbara and Robert, for instance, both have jobs with a high-paying motor vehicle parts manufacturer. Barbara earns just over $23,000; Bob makes $28,000.

Women working on factory assembly lines make up only 4 percent of class A assemblers, the highest-paid group of workers. But they comprise 70 percent of the class C assemblers, the lowest-paid group. Among machine tool operators the relationship is the same. Two percent of the highest group are women; 35 percent are in the lowest-paid group.

Among government workers, too, women are crowded in certain categories at the bottom of the pay scale, whereas men are found in the high-paying jobs. Seventy-five percent of all women are on the lowest federal salary grades (GS-5

NUMBER AND PERCENT OF WOMEN IN FULL-TIME FEDERAL WHITE-COLLAR EMPLOYMENT, BY GENERAL SCHEDULE AND EQUIVALENT GRADES, OCTOBER 31, 1980

General schedule grade[1]	Total employment	Women		
		Number	Percent distribution	As a percent of total
Total, all pay systems[2]	1,985,057	767,117	100.0	38.6
GS and equivalent	1,472,887	663,962	100.0	45.1
01 ($7,960–$9,954)	3,133	2,324	0.4	74.2
02 (8,951–11,265)	17,454	13,284	2.0	76.1
03 (9,766–12,700)	82,989	63,095	9.5	76.0
04 (10,963–14,248)	173,339	133,934	20.2	77.3
05 (12,266–15,947)	194,082	137,894	20.8	71.0
06 (13,672–17,776)	90,349	65,543	9.9	72.5
07 (15,193–19,747)	135,022	72,158	10.9	53.4
08 (16,826–21,875)	31,048	16,198	2.4	52.2
09 (18,585–24,165)	162,421	66,367	10.0	40.9
10 (20,467–26,605)	28,782	10,774	1.6	37.4
11 (22,486–29,236)	165,558	40,214	6.1	24.3
12 (26,951–35,033)	169,239	24,246	3.7	14.3
13 (32,048–41,660)	117,931	11,228	1.7	9.5
14 (37,871–49,229)	64,186	4,316	0.7	6.7
15 (44,547–57,912*)	34,767	2,274	0.3	6.5
16 (52,247–66,183*)	1,848	77	(3)	4.2
17 (61,204–69,364*)	643	29	(3)	4.5
18 (71,734*)	96	7	(3)	7.3

[1] The grades or levels of the various pay systems have been considered equivalent to specific general grade solely on the basis of comparison of salary rates.

[2] Excludes employees of Central Intelligence Agency, National Security Agency, Board of Governors of Federal Reserve System, and foreign nationals overseas.

[3] Less than 0.05 percent.

* The rate of basic pay was limited by Federal regulations.

Source: U.S. Office of Personnel Management, Work Force Analysis and Statistics Division.

ROTHCO

"Our token black—is that really how you think of
yourself, Ms. Corwin? You're much more than that,
I assure you. You're also our token woman."

or below) and earn the lowest wages. Ninety-nine percent of all government secretaries and of all public health nurses are women. Only 6 percent of the women hold jobs on the well-paid administrative level.

Minority women suffer most in the job market. Black women workers, employed full-time, are more likely than others to be in low-paying occupational categories. They are limited both by fewer jobs to choose from and by restricted opportunities. The fields in which large numbers of black women are employed are particularly low paying. For example, the average annual salaries for private household workers is $5,600; waitresses, $7,800; child care workers, $7,900; and retail sales clerks, $9,300.

Even when women get into higher-paying occupations, they are not assured of high wages. Studies have shown that as women enter occupations in large numbers, the wages for that occupation decline. A 1981 National Academy of Science study noted that "the more an occupation is dominated by women, the less it pays." They found that for each additional percentage point of women in an occupation, the average pay in that job is $42 a year lower.

The situation with radio operators illustrates this point very well. In 1960 only 17 percent of all radio operators were women. By 1980 this figure rose to 57 percent. During this twenty-year period, however, the median annual wages in the field dropped sharply. It went from a high of 8 percent above average men's wages in all occupations down to a low of 33 percent below average men's wages.

Over the past decade a number of women have succeeded in breaking barriers against women doing certain kinds of work. They have entered such professions as medicine, law, and engineering, which were traditionally limited to men. But even here they are clustered within the lowest-paid positions in these fields.

Women sometimes lack the training and job experiences needed to qualify for more responsible jobs. The employer is then able to claim that no "qualified" women can be found to fill the higher-paying job openings. As a result, the women remain in the same segregated categories. And the men move up through promotion and advancement.

The latest kind of occupational segregation to enter the work place has been in the fields of computers and high technology. Women have been hired in great numbers to "work with computers." The jobs sound interesting and glamorous at first but often prove to be monotonous. Usually, they offer little chance for advancement. And more often than not, the more challenging computer jobs, such as programming or systems analysis, go to men.

EQUAL PAY FOR
EQUAL WORK

Unequal pay for women and men who perform jobs that are substantially the same is the most widely practiced form of discrimination in the work place. Most societies place a higher value on men's work than on women's work. Where men and women work at jobs requiring similar skills, responsibilities, effort, and work experience, the women are usually paid less than the men.

The government has passed laws to try to end this unfair practice. The Equal Pay Act of 1963 requires that men and women receive equal pay for equal work. Title VII of the Civil Rights Act of 1964 orders an end to discrimination in employment practices, including wages. Yet women still usually earn less than men when they perform jobs that are virtually the same.

One glass manufacturing company, for instance, was paying female packers 25 cents an hour less than male packers. The employers said that the men were paid more because they did extra chores, such as lifting and stacking cartons and using hand trucks. According to the Equal Pay Act, the company was acting illegally. The word *equal*, the court ruled, does not mean identical but only substantially equal. Minor differences in duties cannot be used as an excuse for lower wages.

It is against the law to give unequal pay for equal work. But some employers try to dodge the issue by using different titles for essentially the same job. In some restaurants the man is called chef, the woman doing the same work is called cook; the man is the maitre d', the woman is a hostess. In the office the man is an administrative assistant, the woman, a secretary. In the hospital the man is an orderly, the woman is a nurse's aide. In the hotel the man is a porter, the woman is a chambermaid. And in almost every one of these cases the man's title carries with it a higher pay scale than the woman's. Of course, if the work is essentially the same, the practice is illegal.

Earnings studies of men and women show that the most highly paid occupations for women are about the same as those for men. However, the median earnings of women in these occupations are much lower than for men. This is true in such high-income occupations as lawyers, computer systems analysts, health administrators, engineers, physicians and dentists, elementary and secondary school administrators, personnel and labor relations workers, and operations and systems analysts. Unlike the low-paying occupations, these jobs are male dominated. For example, only 14 percent of physicians and 36 percent of elementary and secondary school administrators are women.

The median annual earnings in the top twenty occupations for women range from a high of $21,944 for operations and systems analysts to a low of $16,536 for librarians. The female operations and systems analysts earn only slightly more than male electricians. The occupation of electrician, though, is well below the top twenty on the male ranking scale. Women librarians' pay is just above that of men working as precision machine operators. Yet such operators are classified in the bottom one-third of male earnings.

Also, the pay differences tend to be greater in the higher-paying than in the lower-paying jobs. Among the greatest differences are the 82 percent gap between male and female operations and systems analysts and the 64 percent salary gap between male and female personnel and labor relations workers.

Some people argue that it is different skills, not sex discrimination, that is to blame for the wage gap in employment. In 1982 Paula England, Marilyn Chasie, and Linda McCormack looked into this idea. They made a study of the four thousand jobs listed in the Department of Labor's *Dictionary of Occupational Titles*. First they rated the jobs by the skills required. Then they grouped them into male and female categories. The results showed very similar skill needs among jobs in both categories yet quite different earnings.

Other studies have compared the productivity levels of men and women. Even in fields where men's productivity was 8 to 20 percent higher than women's, the earnings difference between the sexes was as great as 40 percent.

Women may earn less than men because many interrupt their careers to raise families. Or they may earn less because they leave their jobs when their husbands need to move for a better position. But what of women who devote the same time and effort to the job as men? In a 1982 study Ronald G. Ehrenberg and Robert S. Smith compared the wages of men and women who never married. They found that the average income of women aged twenty-five to sixty-four who never married is still only 65 percent of the average income of men of the same age.

Discrimination in the work place that affects the equal pay issue takes many shapes and forms. *Neutral rule* is a term that lawyers use to refer to job qualifications that appear, on the surface, to be fair and treat both sexes equally but in fact discriminate against women. The neutral-rule doctrine was declared illegal in the 1977 *Dothard v. Rawlinson* Supreme Court decision. At question was the state of Alabama requirement that prison guards had to be at least five feet two inches tall and weigh one hundred twenty pounds.

At first glance this rule may seem neutral. But it is not. According to the rule, 41 percent of all women cannot even be considered for the job. This compares unfavorably with the only 1 percent of men who are ineligible. The state argued that height was a measure of strength, which was necessary for satisfactory job performance. The court ruled against the state, though. It said that they should devise specific tests of the needed strengths and not use this indirect method.

The defeat of the neutral-rule doctrine does not mean that tests may not be used before hiring someone. It just holds that the tests must be a true predictor of who will do a better job. This is called validating the test. A valid test is one that can help to select the best people for a job without failing a disproportionately high percentage of one particular group of people.

Many job-qualifying systems contain a built-in bias or prejudice against women. Height and weight qualifications were once used to keep women out of police work and jobs with the fire department. These jobs were usually thought of as men's jobs. "Now physical strength tests have become the means of determining whether women are fit for non-traditional jobs," says Isabelle Katz Pinzler, director of the American Civil Liberties Union Women's Rights Project.

In 1978 Brenda Berkman was one of seventy-nine women who took a physical test to qualify to become New York City firefighters. All seventy-nine failed. Brenda sued, claiming the test discriminated against women. Under Title VII of the Civil Rights Act of 1964 the tests must be proved to be a valid predictor of job success. If a disproportionate number of women fail a qualifying test, the employer has to show that the test really predicts performance on the job.

The court found in Ms. Berkman's favor. The judge said that the test did not accurately predict actual on-the-job performance. He ordered the city to devise a new examination. Later forty-one women passed and were sworn into the 1982 class of firefighters.

The Equal Pay Act of 1963 and Title VII of the Civil Rights Act of 1964 make it unlawful to pay women less than men for the same job. But men and women seldom hold identical jobs with the exact same job titles. As long as the two sexes are in slightly different job situations, they are not protected by these laws. That is why there is now growing pressure, not for more laws guaranteeing equal pay for equal work but for laws guaranteeing equal pay for work of comparable value to the employer.

EQUAL PAY FOR WORK
OF COMPARABLE WORTH

The goal of equal pay for work of comparable worth is also called pay equity. It means that jobs requiring approximately the same training, experience, responsibility, and so on, should pay the same wages. The jobs of nurses and pharmacists, for example, require similar education and experience and involve similar responsibilities. Yet nurses (most of whom are women) earn an average of $17,300 a year; pharmacists (most of whom are men) have an average salary of $25,000.

In New York City kindergarten teachers need to be college graduates; there is no educational requirement for zookeepers. Yet the starting salary for kindergarten teachers (mostly women) is $14,500, while zookeepers (mostly men) start at a salary of $19,343. Attorney Winn Newman said that across the United States "barbers get more than beauticians, and zookeepers get more than people who take care of children."

A classic case of comparable worth was tried in 1981. Alberta Gunther and three other prison guards at Oregon's Washington County Jail sued (*County of Washington* v. *Gunther*), arguing that they were being paid less than the male guards. They showed that the highest-paid women earned less than the lowest-paid men. The county said that the wage difference was due to the fact that the men guarded more prisoners and the women did more clerical work. But an outside expert showed something else. Although the women did approximately 95 percent of what the men did, they received only 70 percent of their pay.

The Supreme Court found in the women's favor. It ruled that wage discrimination based on sex is unlawful under Title VII of the Civil Rights Act of 1964. The decision helped establish the doctrine of equal pay for jobs of comparable worth to the employer.

Katrina Cannon flexes her muscle after being
sworn in as a firefighter. In 1982, she was one
of forty-one women who broke the sex barrier
of the New York City Fire Department.

But the decision did not answer the all-important question: How do you prove the worth of comparable jobs?

The first step usually is to gather a lot of information about the job from the employees. The process is called job analysis. Experts question the workers about their skills, effort, responsibility, and working conditions. They try to find out as much as they can about the stresses and strains of the job.

At present about fifteen states are trying to find new ways of classifying jobs and correcting unfair pay schedules. In New York they are asking groups of state employees such questions as: How many people are you responsible for? How often do you have to travel overnight on the job? How much time do you spend working under deadlines? Do you do the same things every day?

The second part of the process is to set standards of worth for each job title. This often involves assigning a point value to various job-related factors. For instance, a job that required the ability to use a computer might be rated 10 points, a job where the worker needed only to operate a typewriter would rate 5, and a clerk who did filing would rate 1. Lifting heavy weights daily would rate 10; occasional heavy lifting would be 5; and no lifting would be 0. The manager of an entire plant would get a 10; the supervisor of a small group within the plant would be 5; and someone with no supervisory responsibility would rate 0. After adding up all the points, the worker with the highest total would be paid the highest salary.

The evaluation system, then, tries to make wage scales fairer. It makes it possible, for example, to compare the job fatigue of a bricklayer with that of a nurse, the skills of a stenographer with those of a plumber, the risks in being a taxi driver with those of being a social worker.

Nonetheless, several studies show that the tasks in women's jobs tend to be rated lower than the others. When deciding which factors to include in a job evaluation and what points they should have, the skills involved in a women's job may be given less importance. Speed, fine motor requirements, and adapting to new techniques (characteristic of many clerical occupations) are often given low priority. Taking care of people is less valued than operating machines, and occasional heavy lifting is more highly rated than repeated light lifting.

Sexual prejudice plays a part in job evaluations too. Not long ago chairmen of several college psychology departments were sent descriptions of candidates for teaching positions and asked which they would hire. The only hitch was that the men's and women's names were reversed. The results showed that those with men's names were chosen 10 percent more often than those with women's names, even though they had similar qualifications.

Even after the job evaluation is completed, the amount of wages paid may still favor men. In 1974 the state of Washington hired an outside firm to study the pay differences between men and women. They found that the so-called female jobs, receiving the same or more points than male jobs, were still paying between 22 and 35 percent less.

Two years later the same firm was called in to work out a fair salary structure. They uncovered some shocking examples of unfair wages. The job of park ranger (mostly male) was rated 181 points and was paid on salary level 24; homemaker I (female) was rated 182, yet was paid on salary level 19. Chemist II (male) received 277 points and was listed on salary level 33; registered nurse IV was rated much higher at 573, yet was paid two salary steps lower, on level 31.

In an early case, *Hodgson* v. *Brookhaven General Hospital* (1970), the court decided that male orderlies and female nurses' aides had jobs of comparable worth, even though there were some differences in their duties. The court set up three conditions that would determine if two jobs *did not* have comparable worth: if a special effort was associated with one of the jobs, if this special effort was a significant part of one of the jobs, and if a job had a major economic importance.

In the 1983 case of *American Federation of State, County and Municipal Employees (AFSCME)* v. *State of Washington*, Judge Jack Tanner made a landmark ruling. It was based on evidence that showed that for each percentage increase in the number of women in a job category, there was a corresponding drop in wages for that job. The wages

COMPARISON OF MEDIAN EARNINGS OF YEAR-ROUND FULL-TIME WORKERS, BY SEX, 1955–81
(Persons 15 years of age and over)

Year	Median earnings Women (1)	Median earnings Men (2)	Earnings gap in dollars (3)	Women's earnings as a percent of men's (4)	Percent men's earnings exceeded women's (5)	Earnings gap in constant 1967 dollars (6)
1981	$12,001	$20,260	$8,259	59.2	68.8	$3,032
1980	11,197	18,612	7,415	60.2	66.2	3,004
1979	10,151	17,014	6,863	59.7	67.6	3,157
1978	9,350	15,730	6,380	59.4	68.2	3,267
1977	8,618	14,626	6,008	58.9	69.7	3,310
1976	8,099	13,455	5,356	60.2	66.1	3,141
1975	7,504	12,758	5,254	58.8	70.0	3,259
1974	6,772	11,835	5,063	57.2	74.8	3,433
1973	6,335	11,186	4,851	56.6	76.6	3,649
1972	5,903	10,202	4,299	57.9	72.8	3,435
1971	5,593	9,399	3,806	59.5	68.0	3,136
1970	5,323	8,966	3,643	59.4	68.0	3,136
1969	4,977	8,227	3,250	60.5	68.4	3,435
1968	4,457	7,664	3,207	58.2	65.3	2,961
1967	4,150	7,182	3,032	57.8	72.0	3,079
1966	3,973	6,848	2,875	58.0	73.1	3,032
1965	3,823	6,375	2,552	60.0	72.4	2,958
1964	3,690	6,195	2,505	59.6	66.8	2,700
1963	3,561	5,978	2,417	59.6	67.9	2,637

Year						
1962	3.446	5.974	2.528	59.5	73.4	2.790
1961	3.351	5.644	2.293	59.4	68.4	2.559
1960	3.293	5.417	2.124	60.8	64.5	2.394
1959	3.193	5.209	2.016	61.3	63.1	2.308
1958	3.102	4.927	1.825	63.0	58.8	2.108
1957	3.008	4.713	1.705	63.8	56.7	2.023
1956	2.827	4.466	1.639	63.3	58.0	2.014
1955	2.719	4.252	1.533	63.9	56.4	1.911

Note: For 1967–81 data include wage and salary income and earnings from self-employment; for 1955–66, data include wage and salary income only. For 1979–81, data are for persons 15 years of age and over; earlier data are for persons 14 years of age and over.

Column 3 = column 2 minus column 1.

Column 4 = column 1 divided by column 2.

Column 5 = column 2 minus column 1, divided by column 1.

Column 6 = column 3 divided by the purchasing power of the consumer dollar (1967 = $1.00)

Sources: U.S. Department of Commerce, Bureau of the Census; and U.S. Department of Labor, Bureau of Labor Statistics.

did not appear to be set according to current "market rates" for jobs. Deliberate discrimination, the judge said, was responsible for the failure to raise the pay for those jobs.

Judge Tanner directed that formulas be worked out to raise the pay of the state's women workers. This means that fifteen thousand women working for the state of Washington were ordered to receive pay increases because their jobs are comparable to highly paid jobs held by men. It was the biggest victory so far for the movement to win equal pay for work of comparable worth. The decision is currently being appealed.

Those who challenge the decision claim that it would be very costly for the state of Washington and other states to pay men and women equally. Attorney Winn Newman, who won the *AFSCME* v. *State of Washington* case, agrees that ending discrimination costs money. But he insists that it must be done simply because discrimination is illegal.

Gradually, though, employers are finding that it may cost more to continue the unfair practices than to correct the inequities. The case of the Minnesota State University system is a good illustration. The state legislature discovered that the amount of money needed to defend the unfair salaries in court would exceed the sum necessary to make women's salaries comparable with men's. So it passed a bill establishing a process and timetable for closing the wage gap. The final cost represented less than 4 percent of the total amount of all the state salaries.

Joy Ann Grune is a private consultant on the issue of comparable worth. She says that existing male-female occupational segregation will end when employers will have less "incentive" to have sex-segregated jobs. The remedy, she believes, is comparable worth and the enforcement of existing labor and antidiscrimination laws.

LAWS CONCERNING
FAIR WAGES

The right of women to pay equity is set out in three basic laws. The most important is Title VII of the Civil Rights Act of 1964, which makes pay discrimination based on sex illegal. The Equal Pay Act of 1963 also requires employers to pay men and women the same when they do the same work. And Executive Order 11246, amended by Executive Order 11375, prohibits government contractors and subcontractors from discriminating in hiring.

Most efforts of women to get rid of unfairness in wages depend on Title VII. In 1980 the Supreme Court ruled that wage discrimination based on sex can be tried under Title VII (County of Washington v. Gunther). The law applies even where the jobs are not exactly the same.

The Equal Employment Opportunity Commission (EEOC) is the federal agency that administers Title VII. The EEOC investigates the charges of sex discrimination in the workplace. Or it turns the case over to the state or local agency that handles such complaints.

If the EEOC finds evidence of discrimination under Title VII, the commission tries to correct the problem. The process is known as conciliation. Sometimes the employer does not cooperate. Then the EEOC gives the woman or group of women a "notice of right to sue." The notice can later be used to start a court case against the employer. In June 1985, however, the EEOC set back the struggle for pay equity by ruling that unequal pay for comparable jobs is not proof of discrimination.

The Equal Pay Act requires that women be paid as much as men when they are doing the same work. But it took a number of court cases to arrive at a working definition of "same work." The term now means that the men and women must work at the same place, in a single location. Their jobs must require the same skill, effort, and responsibility. The working conditions must be the same. And finally, the tasks they perform must be exactly or virtually the same.

Over the years a number of jobs have been found to be the same under the Equal Pay Act. Among the better-known ones are orderlies and nurse's aides in hospitals, assembly line workers in factories (even if the men do occasional heavy lifting), and janitors and maids working for colleges. The Equal Pay Act, which is also administered by the EEOC, is quite narrow. It applies only to situations where men and women are doing the same work for different wages. Title VII covers many more kinds of discrimination.

Executive Order 11246 was issued by President Lyndon Johnson and has the effect of a law passed by Congress. In its first form E.O. 11246 required employers who sign contracts with the federal government not to practice race discrimination. The amendment, E. O. 11375, also prohibited sex discrimination. Under these executive orders, any contractor getting a contract for $10,000 or more must agree to an Equal Employment Opportunity clause in the contract. The clause forbids discrimination "because of race, color, religion, sex, or national origin."

The executive orders also require the employer to take "affirmative action" to insure fair labor practices. Hiring policies, promotions and demotions, recruiting, pay scales, and selection for training programs are some affirmative action techniques that are used to treat women as equals of men. If charged with discrimination, firms with fifty or more employers and $50,000 or more in government contracts must put forward an affirmative action plan.

The executive orders are carried out by the Department of Labor's Office of Federal Contract Compliance Programs (OFCCP). From time to time the OFCCP reviews the labor practices of government contractors. If a worker or a group files a complaint, the case is turned over to the EEOC. If the contractor is found to be discriminating, the OFCCP has two main courses of action. It can withhold government payments, or it can turn the case over to the Justice Department for prosecution. In reality, though, the OFCCP rarely takes any action.

In 1982 Minnesota passed a law requiring that pay equity be the most important factor in setting wages for state employees. It also put into effect a comparable-worth system that attempts to eliminate wage discrimination between female- and male-dominated job categories. The Minnesota system, among others, is based on a job study that evaluates the skills and abilities needed to perform various jobs.

In Minnesota the state legislature earmarked $21 million for pay equity adjustments. The sum benefits some 9,000 state employees. The increase will be sizable for many workers. To take only one example, the hourly pay for clerk IIs will increase 23 percent.

LABOR UNIONS
AND FAIR WAGES

Labor unions fight for pay equity through their negotiations with employers. Collective bargaining has won wage equity for state employees in Illinois, Connecticut, and Wisconsin, and for city employees in Los Angeles, Spokane, Washington, and Portland, Oregon. Library workers, clerical personnel, word processing operators, and nurses are a few of those in segregated occupations who have scored pay equity victories through union contract negotiations.

Unions also improve pay equity in other ways. They use anti-sexual-discrimination language for wages, hours, or other conditions of employment. They insist that job openings be posted fairly. And they work to eliminate job titles that artificially separate essentially equal jobs.

By bargaining for dollar, rather than percentage, increases, unions try to bring up the low-wage categories. For example, a 10 percent increase for a $15,000 job comes to $1,500 but only $500 for a $5,000-a-year job. An increase of $1,000 for both jobs costs the employer the same amount yet helps to lessen the gap between the two.

On January 23, 1985, the clerical and technical workers at Yale University successfully ended a ten-week strike on the equal pay issue. Members of the union, the Federation of University Employees, approved a contract that gave large salary increases and other benefits to workers in mostly female job categories. Yale's female clerical and technical workers had been averaging $13,500 a year in salary. They won a 30 percent increase in their salaries over the next three and one-half years.

The Yale contract is the first successful drive for pay equity involving a major employer in the private sector. Most others involved state or federal levels of government. The decision is expected to affect other private employers of clerical workers.

At the union office someone tacked a note on the bulletin board. It was a note that a union bargainer's son left on the kitchen table one evening. It read: "Dad: Mom went to a union meeting." The note symbolizes the fact that women are entering the workplace in increasing numbers. And it is also a symbol of the fact that many women are joining unions to win their demands.

SUMMARY

Government legislation, individual efforts, and the bargaining activities of labor unions are gradually upgrading wages and freeing job titles from discrimination based on sex. Many people in America look forward to a time when all forms of pay discrimination will be part of history.

III

SOCIAL SECURITY, PENSIONS, AND OTHER BENEFITS

Annual Average	Men	Women
Social Security retirement	$5,160	$3,696
Private retirement pension	4,152	1,340
Public retirement pension	4,830	2,750
Total retirement income	8,173	4,757

The average annual retirement income for women, including Social Security and pensions, is little more than half of that of men.

A married woman who works outside the home and pays Social Security taxes may receive no more money in her retirement years than if she had never worked for pay.

A widow has no Social Security income during the so-called widow's gap, the years between the time her youngest child turns sixteen and the time the woman turns sixty (unless she is disabled).

A homemaker who becomes disabled is not eligible for Social Security benefits, even though her disability could cause economic hardship for her family.

About 50 percent of employed men are covered by pension plans. Only 31 percent of employed women have such benefits.

Few private insurance companies will sell disability insurance to a homemaker. Those that do often charge the woman more than the man and pay her lower benefits.

Only 44 percent of women workers who head families are covered by a pension plan at work; only 66 percent of them have health coverage.

Women often pay higher rates for health insurance than men for identical coverage.

After Molly had been working at a textile factory for three years, she had to take a leave of absence to care for her elderly mother. A widow who lived on her Social Security check alone, Molly's mother could not afford to hire a home health aide to prepare her meals and help her dress while she recovered from a bad auto accident.

Seven months later Molly went back to the same company but not the same job. This time she was given a temporary position at a lower salary. It would take her another three years before she would be back on the salary level she was on before her leave. Moreover, she lost all the pension and insurance benefits that she had accumulated during her three years on the job.

Like most working people Molly and her mother depend on various government and private benefit programs to help them get along. In recent years there has been more and more concern over the way women are treated by these various benefit programs. Social Security, pensions, insurance, and maternity benefits are four programs that greatly affect women and their income.

SOCIAL SECURITY

The Social Security Act was passed in 1935. Its basic purpose was to insure certain workers against loss of employment income through retirement. By now it covers 90 percent of all jobs. It gives benefits to insured workers and their dependents on retirement, death, or disability due to illness or injury.

The Social Security tax is paid equally by the employer and the employee. The benefits were never meant to be the primary source of income for retired people. Yet more men and women over the age of sixty-five now receive these benefits than any other type of income. Fifty-two percent of those who receive Social Security are women, 35 percent are men, and 13 percent are children. Although women depend more on Social Security than men do, the benefits they receive are lower.

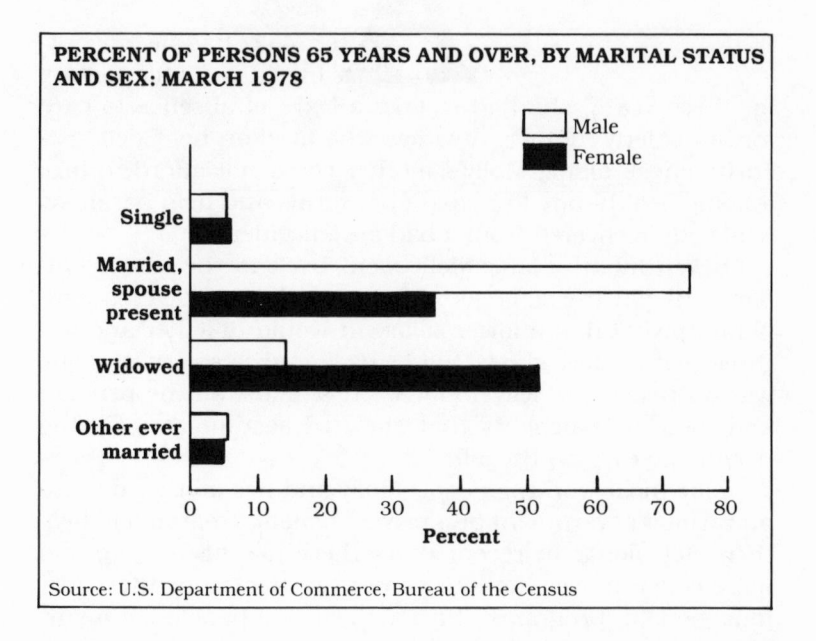

PERCENT OF PERSONS 65 YEARS AND OVER, BY MARITAL STATUS AND SEX: MARCH 1978

☐ Male
■ Female

Single
Married, spouse present
Widowed
Other ever married

Percent

Source: U.S. Department of Commerce, Bureau of the Census

In general, full retirement benefits go to persons at age sixty-five who have worked at a job that is covered by Social Security for at least ten years. Legislation passed in 1983, though, raises the retirement age for Social Security to age sixty-six in the year 2009 and to age sixty-seven in 2027. Dependents (a spouse aged sixty-two or over, a child under age 16, or a wife caring for a child under sixteen) of a retired or disabled worker are also eligible for Social Security benefits.

Women who leave the work force for homemaking responsibilities do not get along very well under Social Security. Every year that they do not work for pay brings down their total Social Security benefit. Homemakers also have no credits to use toward their own Social Security if they later return to work.

Women who have been out of the labor force while caring for the family often lose out on disability benefits, too, under this system. A disability can be any physical or mental handicap that prevents someone from doing his or her job. To qualify for disability benefits a worker must be covered for three months of each year from the age of twenty-one. The worker must also have worked five of the last ten years before the start of disability. This means that women who leave and then reenter the labor force may not receive disability benefits.

When a male worker dies, his wife and children are eligible for survivor's benefits. The widow gets benefits equal to three-fourths of the deceased husband's benefits if she has children under the age of sixteen. But these benefits stop when the youngest child reaches age sixteen. From then until she is sixty (the "widow's gap") the woman receives no income. Starting at sixty she can receive lower benefits. Or she can wait until she is sixty-five and collect the full amount.

Under Social Security a divorced wife has the right to get dependent's benefits if she had been married for ten years. But this, too, puts women at a disadvantage. First, the amount is usually not enough to maintain a separate household. Second, most divorces occur before ten years of marriage. And finally, many women stay home to raise children in the early years of marriage, thereby losing the opportunity to build a Social Security record of their own.

A wife is able to get her own benefits if she worked and paid Social Security taxes for ten years. But often she can get more money as her husband's dependent than as an individual worker. The result is that the wife does not get the benefits for which she was taxed.

Under the law a working wife can receive only one benefit. For this reason many married women with jobs pay Social Security taxes for benefits that nonworking wives receive without being taxed.

Couples with two incomes think it unfair that they may actually receive fewer benefits than one-earner couples with the same average earnings. For example, take two imaginary couples of the same ages: Betty and George, Helen and Tom. Before she married George, Betty worked only a short while. It was not long enough to qualify for Social Security benefits. George earned an average of $18,000 a year during his working life. When he retired, he received $7,608 a year benefits. As his dependent Betty received $3,804 (half as much), for a total of $11,412.

With Helen and Tom it was slightly different. Helen also worked only briefly before marrying Tom, but she went back to work after their children entered school. Her average yearly earnings were $6,300. Tom's average wages were $18,000, exactly the same as George's. Both couples retired at the same time. Tom got the same $7,608 as George, but for all the taxes she paid, Helen received only $3,864—just $60 a year more than Betty, who did not work.

Now suppose Helen and Tom were divorced after six years. Tom remarried; his wife did not work. Helen did not remarry; she continued working until retirement. At retirement, Tom and his new wife would receive $11,412 (his $7,608 plus her $3,804 as his dependent). Helen, though, would receive only $3,864 as a covered worker, about half that of her former husband.

Let's take a third couple, Cathy and John. Each worked and earned an average of $9,000 per year, a total income of $18,000. On retirement each received annual benefits of $4,728, a total of $9,456. This amount is 20 percent less than Betty and George, the one-earner couple, would receive, with exactly the same income.

Many of the problems with Social Security are believed to be the result of changing life-styles. In the typical, average family of 1935, when the law was passed, most husbands were the sole support of the family. Eighty-six percent of the wives were truly dependents. They stayed home to raise the children. Today a majority (55 percent) of women participate in the labor force outside the home. In 1935 approximately one out of six marriages ended in divorce. Today the rate is roughly one out of two. Life expectancy fifty years ago was approximately sixty-five years. Today it is about seventy-five.

Some proposals have been made to correct the shortcomings in the Social Security system as it affects women. One plan would put a value on homemaking or time spent in child care and provide Social Security credits accord-

"No, she wouldn't be interested in a job.
She hasn't worked since we got married."

ingly. Homemakers would pay Social Security taxes similar to those paid by the self-employed. The exact way is yet to be determined. Later they would receive benefits on disability or retirement. In this way women working in the home would take part in the Social Security system just like women who earn a living in the workplace.

Another idea for change has to do with the earnings-sharing for couples. Under this system the family income would belong to both the husband and the wife. Each would get the benefits that come with that income, including Social Security. This plan is based on the belief that marriage is partly an economic partnership. It regards the work of each spouse as of equal value, whether it is done in or outside the home.

The earnings-sharing reform concept has very wide support. It has been backed by the 1979 Advisory Council on Social Security, the 1980 President's Commission on Pension Policy, the 1980 Justice Department's Task Force on Sex Discrimination, and most major women's organizations. A 1984 government study, however, raised some objections to the plan. The study said that the plan would reduce benefits for widows and divorced women, would be expensive to put into effect, and would not mesh well with the current Social Security system.

PENSIONS

A pension is the money paid to a worker, whether by private employer or governmental agency, after the worker retires or is disabled. Pensions supplement Social Security benefits. They are, as you can imagine, an important source of income for aged people.

Pensions usually serve men better than they serve women. Fewer women than men receive pensions. Those women who do receive pensions usually get a lower dollar amount. In 1981 the median private pension amounts were $4,152 for men and $1,340 for women. The public pension plans were higher but still paid men an average of $4,830 and women an average of $2,750.

One of the reasons women usually receive lower pension benefits than men do is that they generally earn lower wages. Since the amount of the pension is usually based on wages earned while working, they get lower benefits. Phyllis and Charlie, for example, are two government workers who both retired in 1982. As clerk-typist Phyllis made $13,000; as mailroom supervisor Charlie earned an average salary of $23,000. At sixty-two Phyllis received a federal pension of $7,500; Charlie's was $13,800. Phyllis's pension is lower than Charlie's because she always held lower-paying jobs.

Women like Phyllis also have different employment patterns that affect their pension benefits. To work his way up to supervisor, Charlie moved twice to different states to take better jobs. These moves helped to advance his career. On the other hand, Phyllis had to quit her job and take a new one each time she moved with Charlie. She also had gaps in her employment for maternity leave and to care for her aged parents. And when the children were very young, Phyllis was able to work only part-time. These breaks in her work record cut down the amount of money she accumulated in her pension fund.

Too often pension plan rules unfairly exclude women. Under many private pension plans, for example, the worker must be twenty-five years or older to join. Yet the greatest percentage of working women are between the ages of twenty and twenty-four. These years of work, therefore, can add nothing toward their pension benefits.

The National Federation of Business and Professional Women's Clubs (BPW) is one of several groups trying to improve women's pension rights. BPW is currently asking that certain changes be made regarding pensions.

One change would be to lower the length of time workers must be employed before they qualify for retirement benefits. In an estimated 75 percent of all private pension plans, the person must be with the same company for at least ten years to get a pension. This requirement, called vesting, often deprives women of their rightful pension benefits. As mentioned above, few women workers are able to remain in the same job for so many years at a time. The result is that many cannot collect their pensions at all. In this way the short-term female workers are helping to finance the pensions of the mostly male long-term workers. Lowering the minimum term of employment for vesting would help all workers but particularly women.

The second unfair pension practice is known as integration. In integration the Social Security benefits are figured in when calculating retired workers' pension benefits. The higher the Social Security, the lower the pension. Social Security benefits are proportionately higher for low-salaried workers (mostly women). Therefore, integration actually results in lower women's pensions. Under integration a worker with a low salary may be covered by a private pension yet receive little or no benefit. Calculating the pension benefits without regard to Social Security would protect all low-salaried workers.

Portability is a third area that could use improvement. It is a way of allowing workers to carry pension credits from one job to another. With portability, workers would be able to change jobs without losing their pension protection.

Two recent laws have helped to improve the country's private pension system. The first was the Employee Retirement Income Security Act (ERISA) of 1974. It set minimum standards for pension plans. ERISA was followed in 1984 by the Retirement Equity Act (REA).

REA is of particular help to women. Under most plans the retiree has two major options: to receive the maximum payment during retirement, with no payments going to the survivor after the retiree's death, or to receive somewhat lower payments on retirement but with monies continuing to be paid to the survivor. The REA requires workers who wish to choose the first option to obtain the written permission of their spouses. Written permission lets the women take part in the decision. Now benefits are more likely to be paid to homemakers than formerly.

Another important part of the bill requires payment of benefits to the spouse of a fully vested worker, even if the worker dies before retirement. For example, a husband dies at age forty after eleven years of work. His wife will now be entitled to survivor benefits when she reaches age fifty-five.

The REA also includes the following features: Workers may enter pension plans at age twenty-one, instead of twenty-five as under ERISA. Pension plans cannot consider a one-year maternity or paternity leave as a break in service. Employees may leave employment for five years without losing their benefits. And in divorce cases the court may award husbands or wives part of their spouse's pension as part of the settlement.

Most pension experts agree that REA is a step in the direction of achieving pension equity for women. Ann E. Moss of the Pension Rights Center in Washington estimated that the bill will provide benefits to seventy thousand women over a five-year period, "a whole class of women who never received them before." But there is little doubt that further reform in equalizing jobs and salaries is needed before women's pensions are truly on a par with men's.

Women are generally charged more than men for the same pension plan. The greater cost is said to be justified because, on average, women live longer than men and might collect benefits over a longer period of time. But as Marion Gray, a lawyer for Women's Equity Action League (WEAL) testified before Congress: "I have one life expectancy as an American—I have a longer expectancy as a woman, a shorter life expectancy as someone in a stress-filled position, a longer life expectancy as a nonsmoker, a shorter life expectancy as one who is overweight. There is no reason why our sex should be singled out to penalize me or my female colleagues when we retire. Our sex will not assure us of a longer life, only a life in more straitened circumstances."

Two important court decisions have helped remove the unfair cost feature for women. The first concerned the Los Angeles Department of Water and Power. This agency required women to contribute 15 percent more than men to the pension fund for comparable benefits. In the case of *Manhart* v. *City of Los Angeles* the Supreme Court decided, on April 25, 1978, that this practice was against the law.

Asking women to pay higher pension contributions violated Title VII of the Civil Rights Act of 1964.

In another case, *Arizona* v. *Norris*, the Supreme Court ruled on July 6, 1983, in favor of women. It said that it was in violation of Title VII for pension plans to pay lower monthly benefits to women because of their greater longevity. As Associate Justice Thurgood Marshall wrote in the opinion, "An individual woman may not be paid lower monthly benefits simply because women as a class live longer."

Congress and the courts have come a long way toward establishing the concept of fairness in pensions. Now various groups are pressing for passage of laws forbidding discrimination in insurance. They want laws that will expand the Norris decision to end the practice of basing insurance costs and benefits on sex.

INSURANCE

Insurance is a way of compensating people for certain kinds of losses. Sickness, injury, auto accidents, fire, robbery, and death are some of the misfortunes that are covered by insurance. With insurance a family can have enough money to meet expenses and replace lost income when something terrible occurs.

There are many kinds of insurance. Life insurance provides a sum of money when someone dies. Automobile insurance covers damages that auto owners may cause to themselves, their cars, or other persons and their property. And health and disability insurance covers medical expenses, such as hospital and surgical bills, as well as loss of income through accident or illness.

In all kinds of insurance, people make regular payments, called premiums, to the insurance company. When insured people have a loss that is covered by their insurance, they make a claim. The company then figures out how much money should be paid to the person named in the policy to receive the benefits. That person is known as the beneficiary.

Currently, most insurance companies determine the provisions of their policies on the basis of sex. Most have decided that life insurance is less expensive for women than for men. The reason? Women live longer. Most have decided that auto insurance costs less for women under twenty-five than for men under twenty-five. The reason? Women that age have fewer auto accidents. And most have decided that private health and disability insurance is more costly for women than for men. The reason? Women under the age of fifty-five have higher medical bills than men.

In 1984 two insurance reform bills were introduced into the Congress. The House bill was called the Non-discrimination in Insurance bill and the Senate version was called the Fair Insurance Practices bill. Both would have prohibited all insurance discrimination on the basis of sex. Since neither bill was passed, the debate on the issues continues.

Supporters of insurance reform consider sex discrimination as unjust as discrimination based on race, color, religion, or national origin. Whites tend to live longer than blacks, and Mormons live longer than non-Mormons, they point out. Yet there is no difference in their insurance rates. Likewise, insurance rates should be the same—that is, unisex or sex-blind—for men and women. If anything, rates should be fixed according to such predictable risk factors as smoking, exercising, or amount of driving, not a person's sex.

In August 1983 the National Research Council reported on "the first large study to try to explain the difference in longevity" between men and women. They found that men who "are not killed violently and do not smoke can be expected to live to the same age as women of their same social level." In other words, the difference in longevity between men and women is due more to patterns of behavior than to any inborn traits.

Thus far the insurance companies and others have insisted that sex is an accurate predictor of life expectancy. They say that longevity differences between the sexes cannot be explained by life-style factors alone. The differences in behavior between men and women have become smaller, they point out, yet the mortality differences have widened. One example they mention is that nonsmoking women generally outlive nonsmoking men. Thus, the companies conclude that women are biologically superior to men.

Among the other arguments against correcting the abuses of the past is the high cost of insurance reform to the policy holder. According to Barbara Lautzenheiser, senior vice-president of Phoenix Mutual Life Insurance Company of Hartford, unisex life insurance would require a twenty-five-year-old, nonsmoking woman to pay $150 more for a one-year $50,000 term policy than she now pays. A thirty-five-year-old woman would pay $350 more. And the rate increases in higher age brackets would be even steeper.

As regards auto insurance, women under the age of twenty-five do have fewer auto accidents than men under the age of twenty-five. With unisex rates these women would probably pay more than at present. According to Phyllis Schlafly of the Eagle Forum, unisex tables would raise auto insurance rates for a twenty-three-year-old single woman in Hartford, Connecticut, by $600; in Newark, New Jersey, by $700; and in Philadelphia, by $800 per year.

But the figures used to justify lower life and auto insurance rates based on sex are misleading. The fact is that the sex-based difference narrows with age and disappears by age twenty-five or thirty. Using the insurance industry's figures, backers of sex-blind insurance are able to show that women over age twenty-five will actually save 20 to 30 percent if a fair factor, such as miles driven, is used to set the rates instead of sex.

On September 27, 1984, the Pennsylvania Supreme Court handed down an important ruling. They said that according to the state's Equal Rights Amendment, insurance companies could not base their auto insurance rates on sex. Probably the fifteen other states that have Equal Rights Amendments will now hear cases on sex discrimination in auto insurance.

In contrast with life and auto insurance, health policies

generally cost women more than they do men for identical coverage. According to health insurance company statistics, women have greater hospital costs and longer stays than men. In the words of Kenneth White, vice-president of the Health Insurance Association of America, "Women are the higher-cost sex in health insurance."

In addition to costing more, women's health plans often offer less. Usually they do not include maternity benefits; and if they do, it is extemely expensive. Women usually have to wait longer to get health insurance and then receive benefits for shorter periods than men do. And they usually find it more difficult and expensive to get disability coverage. Only eight states require companies to have disability insurance, and only 40 percent of women are covered.

Marion Gray, a lawyer for WEAL, has pointed out that women at home suffer the most. She said, "Disability insurance is rarely if ever available to women whose jobs are performed at home, although the loss of homemaker and child care services may mean a substantial cost outlay for replacement services."

Unisex health insurance would mostly benefit women who buy individual health insurance policies. This includes part-time workers and those who do not work outside the home. It would not affect the majority of women who are covered by group insurance in their places of employment.

In August 1984 the National Organization of Women (NOW) filed the first major lawsuit to challenge the practice of charging women higher health and disability rates than men. The suit was filed in Superior Court for the District of Columbia. It contends that Mutual of Omaha, the nation's largest provider of individual health insurance, violated the District's 1977 Human Rights Act. Other suits are expected to follow in some of the twenty-six states that have similar laws.

One of the people filing the lawsuit is Vickey Monrean. Mutual offered Monrean a health insurance policy for $1,149. The same policy is available to men for $690. Mutual also offered her a disability insurance policy for $596. The same policy is available to men for $313. If NOW wins the lawsuit, it will be illegal for insurance companies to charge women more than they charge men for the same coverage.

Thus far no state has outlawed sex-based rates for every form of insurance. But the sides are drawn. On one side are those who want to keep the insurance industry essentially the same. They say that women gain because they currently pay less for life and auto insurance. And they claim it would be difficult as well as expensive to correct the current insurance rates.

On the other side are those who believe that unisex rates will help women in the long run. "We have two things to gain with unisex rates," says Pat Reuss, legislative director of WEAL in Washington, D.C. "We have the basic civil rights principle that discrimination on account of sex is illegal in any way, shape or form, and the second gain—a healthier pocketbook."

MATERNITY RIGHTS

The Pregnancy Discrimination Act of 1978 was added to Title VII of the Civil Rights Act of 1964. The act forbids discrimination against women employees because of pregnancy, childbirth, or related medical conditions. Employers cannot refuse to hire a woman because of pregnancy. Nor can the employer fire a pregnant worker, force her to go on leave, or take away seniority or pension credits for maternity leave.

Before the act was passed, many workers were not treated fairly when they were temporarily unable to work due to pregnancy. Even the Supreme Court upheld this discriminatory attitude. In the 1976 *General Electric Company* v. *Gilbert* case it had ruled that an employer could exclude pregnancy as a disability without violating Title VII of the Civil Rights Act of 1964.

But one year later the *Nashville Gas Company* v. *Satty* case was tried before the Supreme Court. This time the outcome helped women. The case involved Nora Satty, who was forced to go on leave because she was pregnant. When she returned to work, she was denied the advantages of the seniority she had earned for her previous service with the company. Seniority refers to the gains a worker gets as a result of being employed in one place for a period of time. Under company policy, workers could keep seniority during absences for disease or disability but not during pregnancy. The Supreme Court said that the policy violated Title VII of the Civil Rights Act of 1964. It unfairly imposed a burden on women that was not imposed on men.

Many labor unions and civil rights and women's groups have been urging lawmakers to include pregnancy in an employee's insurance coverage. The outcome was the 1978 Pregnancy Discrimination Act. The act clearly forbids discrimination in employment because of pregnancy. Mothers-to-be must be provided leave just the same as other employees who are physically unable to perform their jobs.

In June 1983 the Supreme Court extended the terms of the Pregnancy Discrimination Act to the wives of employees. They said that companies had to provide an employee's wife with pregnancy disability coverage equal to other health-related dependency benefits. Otherwise, the companies would be found to be practicing sex discrimination against male employees.

The Pregnancy Discrimination Act was a big step forward for women's rights in the work place. But there is still room for improvement. The United States now defines pregnancy as a disability. Under the law American employers treat pregnancy like any other physical handicap that prevents a person from working. Perhaps one day employers will show special consideration for women workers who take time out from work to bring children into the world and will provide childbearing benefits to both parents.

IV

SEX DISCRIMINATION IN EDUCATION

THE FACTS

Two-thirds of all boys who enter college have a good math background. But fewer than half of the entering girls have taken advanced math. Without these courses, women cannot become high-paid doctors, engineers, architects, or business managers.

Among non-college-bound students most women are enrolled in home economics, health, and office skills programs. Women represent less than 20 percent of the students in trade and industrial programs.

Thousands of jobs will be opening up every year through 1990 in computer science. Boys now outnumber girls two to one in these courses. Yet in low-level computer skill courses, such as data processing and data entry, girls outnumber boys three to one.

Although women earn about half of all college bachelor's degrees, most are in areas usually dominated by women, such as nursing and primary/secondary school teaching. By and large, this training leads to low-paying jobs.

Women earn about half of the master's degrees, but only one-fourth of the Ph.D.'s, and, again, these are in the traditionally female areas.

Nancy and Mike attended the same big-city elementary, junior high and high school. Nancy was considered a bright achiever. She excelled in English, math, and science. Mike was just as bright as Nancy, but he rarely got as high marks.

Nancy's teachers and guidance counselors urged her to take courses in word processing and keypunching. That way, they said, she could get a job as soon as she graduated. Nancy planned to work for a few years until she got married and had children. Her high school counselor seemed to think that these were good goals.

Mike, on the other hand, was told by the same counselor to "think big" about what he wanted to do with his life and his career. He was advised to take more math and science courses and on graduation to enroll in a computer technician training program.

Both Nancy and Mike were hired by the same company. Nancy began at a salary of $4.40 an hour; Mike's hourly wage was $7.75. Now, after two years with the company, Nancy spends all of her worktime in front of a word processor and has received a $1-an-hour raise. She is allowed one ten-minute break twice a day. Her supervisor, who started as a clerk-typist five years ago, earns $8.20 an hour.

Mike's job qualifies him for a management training program offered by the company. He spends half his time as a computer technician and the other half taking management courses. Mike earns $11.30 an hour and takes long lunches with his supervisors.

Even with time out to have a family, most women will work most of their lives. Education, we know, affects the kinds of jobs that one can get. Usually, the more schooling and training you have, the better your chances of getting a good job at a high salary. Yet because high school counselors and teachers often do not encourage girls to pursue career paths, many enter the work force with no special training and with low-paid skills. Frequently they earn less than men from the beginning. And they find it hard to move up the career ladder because of limited training.

Children generally come into school ready and eager to learn. Studies show that very young girls tend to develop reading, counting, and speaking skills more quickly than boys. Most either equal or surpass boys in math and science during the early school years. A 1982 assessment by the National Institute of Education showed that at age nine overall math and science scores for girls were higher than those for boys. At age thirteen, though, the scores for girls and boys were virtually the same.

But high school, it seems, presents changes. Boys tend to take more mathematics and science than girls do, even though similar proportions of each group are enrolled in academic courses. By age seventeen the scores for girls were generally lower than those for boys. Not long ago boys scored an average of 50 points higher than girls did on the math part of the Scholastic Aptitude Test (SAT) given for college entrance.

One theory has it that girls grow up believing that they cannot compete in the math and science fields. Recent research shows that at every age level there are fixed, usually negative views about the role of women in society. And there are some signs that the education system keeps these ideas going.

Elementary school teachers, for example, often treat boys and girls differently in everyday classroom situations. A project funded by the National Institute for Education found that primary school teachers asked the boys "higher order" questions. Also, they encouraged them on more occasions.

The teachers, it was observed, often gave the boys instructions on how to complete a project. With the girls, either they showed them how or did it for them. Boys tended to be praised more often for the intellectual quality of their work and criticized for lack of neatness. Girls were praised more for neatness and less for thinking.

Other studies found that elementary teachers encouraged confidence and leadership qualities in boys, but not in girls. One researcher reported that teachers talked more often to boys than to girls. They addressed remarks to boys no matter where they were in the classroom but to girls only when they were nearby. The conclusion was that girls who get less attention from teachers may grow up with a lower sense of importance.

Patterns in child-rearing practices help set the stage for the kinds of views of themselves that children come to hold. Mary P. Rowe, special assistant to the president at Massachusetts Institute of Technology, calls these daily behaviors directed at children "micro-inequities." Small differences in treatment, she says, affect the learning climate and can have major negative results.

The books and materials used in school also give young people a sense of their own importance. Many readers and textbooks present boys and girls in traditional roles. Boys are frequently portrayed as leaders, achievers, and independent people. Girls are more often shown as dependent, passive observers.

Some researchers trace girls' avoidance of computers to differences in social development and to methods of teaching computer science. Girls at an early age get the idea from television commercials, parents, and friends that computers are for boys. When they get to high school, they find that the computers are in high school math and science departments, usually headed by men. This only makes the male-dominated view of computers that much stronger.

According to one study by Johns Hopkins University, first-grade girls were just as interested as boys in learning to program computers. By sixth grade, however, twice as many boys as girls were interested in computers. By ninth grade more than four-fifths of the interested students were male.

Although sex roles are taught in school, they probably arise first in the family. Parental attitudes are believed to be the most basic influence. The process may well begin in infancy by differences in the way parents handle and treat the very young child.

Many families, for example, provide different toys and games for boys and girls. Customarily, girls receive dolls, tea sets, and other toys that develop social and verbal skills. Boys get mechanical devices to play with and are encouraged to play games that develop manual skills and stress competitiveness.

As children grow up, the image that their parents have of them affects the occupational choices they make. One study followed a group of teenagers and their parents from seventh through twelfth grades. The results showed that as the girls approached graduation from high school their parents attached more and more value to homemaking qualities and a domestic role for them. By the time the girls reached their senior year their career goals were lower than boys' for the first time.

VOCATIONAL EDUCATION

Vocational education has always been a very important way for students to acquire occupational skills for jobs that do not require a college education. Offered mostly in high schools and community and junior colleges, vocational education programs enroll about 40 percent of all high school students and 30 percent of all community college students.

But studies find that vocational schools, too, seem to offer two different kinds of education, one for men and one for women. Less than 1 percent of female students in vocational schools are being trained for the higher-paying technical jobs. But nearly 4 percent are still being taught homemaking skills that produce no wages at all. Of a group of female students taking trade and industry courses, one-third said their teachers and counselors had tried to talk them out of it.

The League of Women Voters Education Fund recently completed a two-year study of vocational education programs in five states: Massachusetts, Pennsylvania, Iowa, Idaho, and Wisconsin. The study found that the sex segregation in vocational training programs closely resembled the occupational segregation of the labor market.

In Massachusetts and Pennsylvania male students were more heavily enrolled than female students in the trade areas—plumbing, electricity, mechanics, and so on. The female students were concentrated in such traditional courses as home economics, horticulture, and cosmetology, and in some less heavily stereotyped classes, such as data processing and commercial art.

In one school district in Pennsylvania female students had to take nine weeks of shop and twenty-seven weeks of home economics. Male students had to take the opposite, twenty-seven weeks of shop and nine weeks of home economics. These requirements illustrate one way women are discouraged from getting the training necessary for entering occupations not usually held by women.

Several laws now require states to take steps to overcome sex discrimination in federally funded vocational education programs. Title IX of the Education Amendments of 1972, an addition to the 1963 Vocational Education Act, prohibits sex discrimination in federally assisted programs and activities. Under the law male students cannot be barred from enrolling in courses such as cooking that have traditionally been female. Neither can girls be stopped from studying typically male subjects such as industrial arts.

Other important statutes affecting vocational education are the Education Amendments of 1976 and 1984. These amendments aim to end occupational segregation in vocational education. They also attempt, through vocational education, to channel women into higher-paying fields not usually open to women.

Weaknesses in the law and in procedures for enforcement may be the cause of some problems in vocational education. The state of Wisconsin, for example, was cited for sex-based discrimination in its vocational education programs. State education officials promised to look into the matter. But according to the League, they failed to follow up on the case.

There are several reasons for low female enrollments in the vocational education programs that prepare students to work in areas not usually open to women. The main ones are said to be: pressure from friends; influence of parents; the attitudes of administrators, teachers, counselors, and industry; and the traditional ways of thinking about male/female roles.

Interviewers in Idaho reported one secondary teacher who said, "It is foolish to think that men and women can do the same job . . . women have better dexterity, men have greater strength." And in Wisconsin several trade and industry instructors stated, "Girls don't want to get dirty." One businessman in Idaho said: "Women are never forced into a job, they are taken care of. Men are forced to provide for their families."

In Iowa, parents were questioned about students' vocational education program choices. About one thousand adults across the state were called and asked how they would react if their teenage son or daughter chose a career that was uncommon for his or her sex—i.e., auto mechanic or farmer for girls, secretary or nurse for boys. "Would you encourage her/him in that field, would you object but allow her/him to do it, or would it not matter?"

Most parents who objected to unusual career choices said that it was because the job in question was a man's or a woman's job. Parents of sons often mentioned the low pay associated with women's jobs. But even where the man's job was low-paying and of low status, few parents gave low pay as a reason for objecting to a daughter's uncommon choice.

The League concluded that there was still a lot of sex discrimination in vocational education. They decided that teachers and counselors need to work harder to treat students in a sex-blind way. The new laws do not seem to be changing attitudes about bringing women into fields where few of them have worked before. Where students did enroll in programs that are considered untraditional for them, they performed well, even without background experience.

APPRENTICESHIP AND
TRAINING PROGRAMS

Apprenticeship is a way of learning to be a skilled craft worker through a combination of on-the-job training and classroom instruction. Apprentices work with master journeyworkers who teach and supervise them in a shop or at a work site. This training goes along with related instruction at a vocational school, trade or technical college, or through a correspondence course.

An important advantage of apprentice training is that the trainees earn money while they learn. Wages for an entering apprentice are about half that of a highly skilled journeyworker, with increases every six months. On completion of the program the apprentice gets a card indicating that he or she is skilled in a specific occupation.

Women are gradually coming into better-paying, traditionally male fields through apprenticeship programs. In 1973, 0.7 percent of the registered apprentices in the country were women. There has been a slight improvement since then; in 1978 the proportion was up to 2.6 percent. In 1973 women were apprenticed in only 70 of the 450 occupations that have apprentice programs. By 1978 they could be found in three hundred of the occupations.

Women have proved that they are interested in blue-collar work (the kind of work done in work clothes) when given a chance to be hired. The city of Seattle, Washington, decided to hire 15 percent of women for city-financed construction and met that goal easily. The Ingalls shipyard in Pascagoula, Mississippi, wanted to put 20 percent of women to work. The number of women working there went from 89 in 1971 to 2,426 in 1978. And as a final example, there is the building of the Alaska pipeline. Over two thousand women, or 11 percent of the work force, worked on the project under the most difficult conditions, as teamsters, laborers, and engineers.

The barriers to women in apprenticeship are the same as in other education programs. The first is sex discrimination. The same old myths operate here as elsewhere, about women's jobs and roles, physical and mental capacities, commitment to the job, and potential conflict with family responsibilities.

Another barrier for women has to do with inadequate preparation for apprenticeship. As we have seen, many women are discouraged from taking shop, mechanical drawing, industrial arts, and other vocational education

Today more and more women are working
in traditionally male occupations.
Shown here are a cameraperson,
telephone lineperson, construction worker,
window washer, and train dispatcher.

courses in high school. They also take fewer of the math and science classes that are required for most apprenticeship programs. Women often find that they have little or no experience with the tools, procedures, language, and duties related to the skilled craft jobs. Often they feel at a disadvantage because they lack the background skills that men may have had from an early age.

The next difficulty is age restriction. This requirement limits apprenticeship opportunities for both women and men in the skilled trades. Some apprenticeship programs require that apprentices must be under twenty-four to twenty-seven years of age on entering. This is a special problem for women, since many women enter apprenticeship after some years of work. They are often in their late twenties or early thirties when they discover what the skilled trades offer. By then they may be turned away for being too old.

Finally, women entering longtime mostly male occupations have to deal with annoying behavior directed at them because they are female. Often name-calling and ridicule are part of the initiation process. Harassment interferes with work, with the opportunity to learn, and with the worker's safety and health. In addition, where women are excluded from the group, it takes them longer to get to "know the ropes." This makes it even harder to master the job.

EDUCATION IN
MILITARY SERVICE

The armed forces have always been an important place for learning valuable skills and training that may not be available elsewhere. Probably that is why since 1972 there has been a steady increase in the number of women in the military. By March 1982, 191,340 women made up 9 percent of all military personnel. Of that number, 39.8 percent were in the Army, 33.8 percent in the Air Force, 22.1 percent in the Navy, and 4.2 percent in the Marines. About 13 percent of the women (24,311) were officers.

Women can now be assigned to all military specialties that are not related to combat. And they are seeking the uncommon fields in greater numbers than ever before. Women can be found in such unusual occupations for them as electronics equipment repair, communications, and intelligence. They are also members of missile crews, pilots of support aircraft, refueling operators, and load masters. Their participation in these job areas has jumped from less than 2 percent in 1971 to almost 50 percent in 1980. Of course, the remaining 50 percent of women in the armed forces continue to do what are considered women's jobs, such as nursing and clerical work.

Many lawsuits have been started to allow women to play a bigger part in the military. Without easy access to these jobs women are losing a valuable training opportunity. The best example, perhaps, is that commercial airlines hire almost all of their pilots from among those trained by the Air Force. The difficulty is that though the military is a major educational source its teaching divisions are exempt from Title IX of the Education Amendments of 1972 Act.

In 1982, for instance, the Army, in addition to banning women from combat jobs, closed twenty-three job categories that they said were combat related. They also barred enlisted female soldiers from entering forty-nine other job specialties. These two groups of specialities represent about 30 percent of all Army jobs. The job closings eliminate many career opportunities for enlisted women. They also threaten the career advance of women officers in these fields. The cuts, the Army said, were not due to any problems with performance.

The military services also differ as to which jobs women can hold. Women can fly jets in the Navy, Army, and Air Force but not in the Marine Corps. Civilian women can sail on support ships with the Navy fleet, yet Navy women cannot sail on those same ships.

COLLEGE EDUCATION

In 1979 women earned most of their college degrees in the fields of home economics (95.1 percent women), library science (94.6 percent), and the health professions (82 per-

Members of an all-female crew
of the U.S. Air Force stand in
front of their C-141B Starlighter
in Frankfurt, Germany.

SCIENCE AND ENGINEERING BACHELOR'S/FIRST PROFESSIONAL DEGREE RECIPIENTS BY FIELD AND SEX: 1970–81

Year	Total S/E	Physical sciences [1]	Engineering
Total			
1970	264,122	21,551	44,772
1971	271,176	21,549	45,387
1972	281,228	20,887	46,003
1973	295,391	20,809	46,989
1974	305,062	21,287	43,530
1975	294,920	20,896	40,065
1976	292,174	21,559	39,114
1977	288,543	22,618	41,581
1978	288,167	23,175	47,411
1979	288,625	23,363	53,720
1980	291,983	23,661	59,240
1981	294,867	24,175	64,068
Men			
1970	195,244	18,582	44,434
1971	198,180	18,535	45,022
1972	203,557	17,739	45,502
1973	211,552	17,688	46,409
1974	213,269	17,751	42,824
1975	201,578	17,058	39,205
1976	196,577	17,420	37,671
1977	191,090	18,067	39,495
1978	188,107	18,188	43,914
1979	186,333	18,076	48,801
1980	186,009	18,010	53,226
1981	186,425	18,195	56,951
Women			
1970	68,878	2,969	338
1971	72,996	3,014	365
1972	77,671	3,148	501
1973	83,839	3,121	580
1974	91,793	3,536	706
1975	93,342	3,838	860
1976	95,597	4,139	1,443
1977	97,453	4,551	2,086
1978	100,060	4,987	3,497
1979	102,292	5,287	4,919
1980	105,974	5,651	6,014
1981	108,442	5,980	7,117

[1] Includes environmental science.
[2] Includes computer specialties.
[3] Includes psychology.

Mathematical sciences[2]	Life sciences	Social sciences[3]
29,109	52,129	116,561
27,306	51,461	125,473
27,250	53,484	133,604
27,528	59,486	140,579
26,570	68,226	145,449
23,385	72,710	137,864
21,749	77,301	132,451
20,729	78,472	125,143
19,925	77,138	120,518
20,670	75,085	115,787
22,686	71,617	114,779
26,406	68,086	112,132
18,593	40,254	73,381
17,488	39,658	77,477
17,466	40,790	82,060
17,543	44,916	84,996
16,851	50,390	85,453
14,729	51,899	78,687
14,071	53,512	73,903
13,241	52,863	67,424
12,815	50,184	63,006
13,249	47,537	58,670
14,439	44,021	56,313
16,672	40,610	53,997
10,516	11,875	43,180
9,818	11,803	47,996
9,784	12,694	51,544
9,985	14,570	55,583
9,719	17,836	59,996
8,656	20,811	59,177
7,678	23,789	58,548
7,488	25,609	57,719
7,110	26,954	57,512
7,421	27,548	57,117
8,247	27,596	58,466
9,734	27,476	58,135

Source: National Center for Education Statistics,
Earned Degrees (annual series)
and National Science Foundation.

SCIENCE AND ENGINEERING MASTER'S DEGREE RECIPIENTS BY FIELD AND SEX: 1970–81

Year	Total S/E	Physical sciences [1]	Engineering
Total			
1970	49,318	5,948	15,597
1971	50,624	6,386	16,347
1972	53,567	6,307	16,802
1973	54,234	6,274	16,758
1974	54,175	6,087	15,393
1975	53,852	5,830	15,434
1976	54,747	5,485	16,170
1977	56,731	5,345	16,889
1978	56,237	5,576	17,015
1979	54,456	5,464	16,193
1980	54,391	5,233	16,846
1981	54,811	5,300	17,373
Men			
1970	40,741	5,101	15,425
1971	41,966	5,533	16,160
1972	44,010	5,419	16,521
1973	44,474	5,427	16,470
1974	43,630	5,200	15,031
1975	42,847	4,982	15,038
1976	42,675	4,660	15,581
1977	43,577	4,458	16,156
1978	42,547	4,630	16,144
1979	40,416	4,472	15,203
1980	40,008	4,258	15,656
1981	39,797	4,213	15,967
Women			
1970	8,577	847	172
1971	8,658	853	187
1972	9,557	888	281
1973	9,760	847	288
1974	10,545	887	362
1975	11,005	848	396
1976	12,072	825	589
1977	13,154	887	733
1978	13,690	946	871
1979	14,040	992	990
1980	14,383	975	1,190
1981	15,014	1,087	1,406

[1] Includes environmental science.
[2] Includes computer specialties.
[3] Includes psychology.

Mathematical sciences[2]	Life sciences	Social sciences[3]
7,107	8,590	12,076
6,789	8,320	12,782
7,186	8,914	14,358
7,146	9,080	14,976
7,116	9,605	15,974
6,637	9,618	16,333
6,466	9,823	16,803
6,496	10,707	17,294
6,421	10,711	16,514
6,101	10,719	15,979
6,515	10,278	15,519
6,787	9,731	15,620
5,298	6,374	8,543
5,101	6,130	9,042
5,409	6,587	10,074
5,416	6,843	10,318
5,323	7,195	10,881
4,871	7,207	10,749
4,776	7,204	10,454
4,730	7,696	10,537
4,704	7,485	9,584
4,469	7,259	9,013
4,715	6,952	8,427
4,939	6,451	8,227
1,809	2,216	3,533
1,688	2,190	3,740
1,777	2,327	4,284
1,730	2,237	4,658
1,793	2,410	5,093
1,766	2,411	5,584
1,690	2,619	6,359
1,766	3,011	6,757
1,717	3,226	6,930
1,632	3,460	6,966
1,800	3,326	7,092
1,848	3,280	7,393

Source: National Center for Education Statistics,
Earned Degrees (annual series)
and National Science Foundation.

SCIENCE AND ENGINEERING DOCTORATE RECIPIENTS BY FIELD AND SEX: 1970—82

Year	Total S/E	Physical sciences [1]	Engineering
Total			
1970	17,743	4,403	3,434
1971	18,948	4,501	3,498
1972	19,009	4,257	3,503
1973	19,001	4,078	3,364
1974	18,313	3,765	3,147
1975	18,358	3,710	3,002
1976	17,864	3,506	2,834
1977	17,418	3,415	2,643
1978	17,048	3,234	2,423
1979	17,245	3,320	2,490
1980	17,199	3,149	2,479
1981	17,623	3,208	2,528
1982	17,614	3,348	2,644
Men			
1970	16,117	4,160	3,419
1971	17,007	4,256	3,483
1972	16,906	3,986	3,481
1973	16,551	3,816	3,318
1974	15,706	3,496	3,114
1975	15,522	3,416	2,950
1976	14,883	3,199	2,780
1977	14,311	3,112	2,569
1978	13,735	2,926	2,370
1979	13,662	2,970	2,428
1980	13,398	2,763	2,389
1981	13,602	2,844	2,429
1982	13,479	2,840	2,520
Women			
1970	1,626	243	15
1971	1,941	245	15
1972	2,103	271	22
1973	2,450	262	46
1974	2,007	269	33
1975	2,836	294	52
1976	2,981	307	54
1977	3,107	303	74
1978	3,313	308	53
1979	3,583	350	62
1980	3,801	386	90
1981	4,021	364	99
1982	4,135	458	124

[1] Includes environmental science.
[2] Includes computer specialties.
[3] Includes psychology.

Mathematical sciences[2]	Life sciences	Social sciences[3]
1,225	4,165	4,516
1,238	4,556	5,155
1,281	4,454	5,514
1,233	4,503	5,823
1,211	4,304	5,886
1,147	4,402	6,097
1,103	4,361	6,110
964	4,266	6,130
959	4,369	6,063
979	4,501	5,955
962	4,716	5,893
960	4,783	6,144
940	4,840	5,842
1,148	3,627	3,763
1,142	3,896	4,230
1,185	3,781	4,473
1,113	3,714	4,590
1,096	3,524	4,476
1,038	3,553	5,565
890	3,508	4,506
837	3,423	4,370
828	3,411	4,200
833	3,470	3,961
846	3,566	3,834
822	3,562	3,945
824	3,552	3,693
77	538	753
96	660	925
96	673	1,041
120	789	1,233
115	780	1,410
109	849	1,532
113	853	1,654
127	843	1,760
131	958	1,863
146	1,031	1,994
116	1,150	2,059
138	1,221	2,199
116	1,288	2,149

Source: National Academy
of Sciences and National
Science Foundation.

cent). Men were best represented in military science (96.5 percent) and engineering (91.7 percent).

Over recent years, though, more women have been choosing programs leading to science and engineering degrees. Women earned only about 26 percent of the bachelor's degrees awarded scientists and engineers in 1970. By 1981 they were getting 37 percent of these degrees. The gain is still considered small though, since women earned almost one-half of all 1981 undergraduate degrees.

The same trend also holds for advanced degrees in science and engineering. The number of such degrees awarded to women rose a remarkable 75 percent in the decade between 1970 and 1981. But even with this great spurt women accounted for only 8 percent of the total number of master's degree recipients and less than 5 percent of those who earned engineering doctorates in 1981.

One difference between men and women is the fact that men get more financial support for their graduate or advanced-degree education than women do. In 1979 only 11.7 percent of the projects that were funded by the National Institutes of Health, for example, were headed by women. Without research money women find it difficult to advance their scientific careers. Today, with less research money available overall, women scientists are feeling the pinch even more than their male colleagues.

A study of students in the late 1970s, called the Report of the Brown Project, set out to find out more about the low college enrollment of women in fields dominated by men. It concluded that "even though men and women are presumably exposed to the same curriculum and programs during their undergraduate years, it seems these programs serve more to preserve, rather than to reduce, stereotypical differences between men and women in behavior, personality, aspirations and achievement."

According to the Brown Report, women undergraduates don't feel as well prepared for graduate school as men attending the same university. Many drop their academic and career goals during their college years. As one female Ph.D. candidate at Harvard said: "You come in the door . . . equal but having experienced the discrimination—the refusal of professors to take you seriously; the sexual overtures and the like—you limp out doubting your own ability to do much of anything."

Another study of college students from about the same time also showed that many women tend to think of themselves not quite on a par with men. This report also says that teachers are partly responsible. Intentionally or not, faculty at colleges and universities may discriminate against women. Especially in areas of study not usually open to women, teachers question the competence as well as commitment of female students. "I told my advisor I wanted to continue working toward a Ph.D.," reported one student. "He said, 'A pretty girl like you will certainly get married. Why don't you stop with an M.A.?' " Another told of a teacher who said, "It doesn't matter if you finish your thesis this year. You probably won't use it for much anyway."

One of the greatest concerns of women college students has to do with those areas that Mary P. Rowe calls microinequities. You may recall these are little negative things that teachers do and say every day that affect the classroom atmosphere. For example, studies find that women are often interrupted while speaking. As a Harvard student put it, "A professor repeatedly cuts off women while in the middle of an answer in class. He rarely does this to men."

This kind of sexual bias in colleges and universities puts women at a disadvantage. It may make women students believe that they are not important members of the class and that their participation is not expected. It may contribute to the high dropout rate of women graduate students. And it may create an impression that women students have a limited capacity for intellectual development. All of these factors influence career goals and later professional success.

We said that work performed by men is usually valued more than work performed by women. But academic achievement by men also may be considered more important than that done by women. The tendency to devalue women and their work can lower self-confidence. As a pro-

Alice Dickinson, Professor of Mathematics Emeritus,
with her students at Smith College.

fessor at Oberlin College said: "I had women students who were very bright and who didn't perceive themselves as such, whereas I had male students who were of moderate capabilities and convinced that their brilliance was going unrecognized."

Most of the women who are entering college today in increasing numbers have a great new sense of their own importance. Many will meet the challenge of academe with talent and creativity. But the problems that remain seem to indicate that more help from the college community is needed.

LEGAL REMEDIES

Several key federal laws are available to fight sex discrimination in education. All students can now have their rights enforced under the equal protection clause of the Fourteenth Amendment to the United States Constitution, the Equal Educational Opportunities Act of 1974, Title IV of the 1964 Civil Rights Act, and the Education Amendments of 1972 (which includes Title IX), 1976, and 1984, which were added to the Vocational Education Act of 1963.

The equal protection clause of the Fourteenth Amendment prohibits discrimination by public schools and colleges. Many important legal battles have been fought against sex discrimination under this clause. One of the most important is the struggle for women to attend all-male schools and for men to attend all-female schools. In recent years women have won the right to be admitted to such prestigious men-only schools as the University of Virginia at Charlottesville, Stuyvesant High School in New York City, Boston Latin School in Boston, and Lowell High School in San Francisco.

In 1982 the Supreme Court ruled that the Mississippi University for Women could not exclude men from its School of Nursing (*Mississippi University for Women v. Hogan*). In writing the Court's opinion Justice Sandra Day O'Connor said that the all-female policy reinforced the image of nursing as a women's field. She also pointed out that an all-female policy may actually harm women, rather than help them, by lowering nurses' wages.

To enforce a person's rights under the equal protection clause, a man or a woman can bring a lawsuit against the discriminating school or official. With the help of a lawyer he or she sues for an injunction, a court order forbidding or calling for a certain action. If the individual wins the decision, the judge may order the school to admit the student. Or the judge can tell the school to stop enforcing a rule that discriminates against men or women. Sometimes the court will award the victim money damages.

The Equal Educational Opportunities Act declares that "all children enrolled in public schools are entitled to equal educational opportunities without regard to race, color, sex, or national origin." But although it includes specific prohibitions against segregation of students and teachers by race, it makes no mention of segregation by sex.

Title IV of the 1964 Civil Rights Act has been used mainly to desegregate public schools. It has not yet been used to fight educational discrimination in integrated schools. But a woman or man may ask the U.S. attorney general to sue a school or college that practices discrimination. At the elementary and secondary school level the parents of children who are involved in discrimination send a letter to the attorney general. College students can raise the complaint themselves. The letter should be sent to Attorney General, U.S. Department of Justice, Washington, D.C. 20530, Att: General Litigation Section, Civil Rights Division.

The Education Amendments of 1976 and 1984 were added to the 1963 Vocational Education Act. Title II of the 1976 amendment requires each state to take steps to end sex discrimination in vocational education. It does not provide a way to punish those who do not comply with the law. But it attempts to put an end to occupational segregation in vocational education programs. The law names experts to check that state vocational education programs do not discriminate against any students.

The famous Title IX of the Education Amendments of 1972 prohibits sex discrimination in federally assisted programs and activities in any school from the preschool level through graduate education. The law forbids excluding a girl or a boy from any class or activity because of sex. The major exceptions are in physical education, sex education, and a chorus selected on the basis of vocal range.

The law, however, does permit discrimination in admission to certain schools. And it considers each school, college, or department of a university that has a separate administration a different educational institution for admissions purposes. It exempts textbooks and other curricular materials from the law because of a possible conflict with the right of freedom of speech and press from government interference.

Since 1979 women and men may bring their own suits in federal court under Title IX against schools that discriminate on the basis of sex. Also, the attorney general can bring such lawsuits. A letter giving details of the discrimination charges should be sent to Assistant Secretary for Civil Rights, Office of Civil Rights, Department of Education, Washington, D.C. 20202.

The chief weaknesses of Title IX are its poor procedures for enforcement and its many loopholes. Experts claim that the Title IX provisions are confused and lead to government inefficiency. It also may be that sex discrimination has a low priority and that is the reason behind the lack of enforcement of this law.

One of the major impacts of Title IX has been in the field of school athletics. Before the 1970s the major part of a school's athletic budget went for the highly visible boys' teams. Girls often had to pay for their own uniforms, travel, and equipment. There were no athletic scholarships available for women.

Since the law's passage in 1972 and the guidelines to it that were passed in 1975, women's teams have started to get their fair share. Uniforms and equipment are now being provided. The schools pay for coaches and travel, and scholarship money is made available. Better conditions for playing and more opportunities to play competitively have vastly improved the quality of girls' athletics. Between 1972 and 1982 the number of girls participating in sports in public high schools grew nearly 118 percent. Many of the women who excelled in the 1984 Olympics received their first opportunities as the result of Title IX improvements in school programs.

On February 28, 1984, though, the Supreme Court made an important Title IX ruling. The effect was to weaken and narrow the law's impact substantially. In the case of *Grove City College* v. *Bell* the court ruled that Title IX applies only to the programs, courses, or activities within a school that are specifically funded by the federal government, rather than to the entire institution. Only 4 percent of the $13 billion of federal funds received each year by colleges and universities is earmarked for specific programs. Therefore, Title IX no longer applies to the remaining 96 percent of school programs. Athletic programs seldom receive federal dollars. Thus, there is no longer any legal requirement for equality in the athletics department.

Within months after the Supreme Court decision several reactions set in. The Office of Civil Rights within the Department of Education dropped twenty-three sex discrimination cases (and is expected to drop others), narrowed the scope of eighteen cases, and decided to review another thirty-one cases. One of the cases involved an institution that was sued by its women athletes for numerous inequities. One of the unfairest practices had to do with sending women athletes on the road to sleep three in a bed, while each male athlete had a bed to himself. Since its athletic program does not receive direct federal funding, the university has asked that the suit be dropped in light of the Supreme Court's decision.

In early 1985 Senator Edward Kennedy helped introduce a reform bill in Congress. The bill makes clear that Title IX's purpose is to prohibit discrimination throughout schools and all other institutions receiving federal funds. The Kennedy bill would restore the wide ban on sex discrimination in education that was originally intended by Title IX. Many groups, including civil rights, women's rights, the aging, handicapped, youth, religious, and education organizations are backing the bill. A rival piece of legislation was introduced by Senator Robert Dole. The Dole bill would apply only to educational institutions. Thus, a college would be covered, but a hospital would not. Senator Dole called his bill a "middle-ground approach."

Currently, each campus can make its own definition of discrimination. If students are victims of sex discrimination in a part of the school not directly funded by Washington, they have no legal recourse. Bernice Resnick Sandler, director of the Project on the Status and Education of Women at the Association of American Colleges, said that in the past victims of sex discrimination in schools could say, "That's illegal." Now all they can say is "That's not nice."

SEXUAL HARASSMENT

THE FACTS

A leading magazine questioned nine thousand clerical and professional women nationwide about sexual harassment at work. Ninety-two percent said they had been subjected to unpleasant and annoying behavior by male workers.

A study of New York working women found that 70 percent had experienced sexual harassment. The vast majority of the cases, however, had not been reported. Fifty-two percent believed nothing would be done. Forty-two percent thought they would be ridiculed. And 30 percent were afraid they would be blamed and suffer as a result.

Arizona State University recently interviewed 1,500 male and female faculty members, students, and staff. Thirteen percent of the women and 5 percent of the men had been sexually harassed on the campus. More than 30 percent of those surveyed said the incident had had a bad effect on them. Faculty members had suffered in their career advancement. Students had received lower grades.

Jane is an accountant who was employed in a mostly male San Francisco investing firm. By and large the men in the office were very nice to work with, but two consultants on the staff constantly annoyed Jane. Each time she had to walk by either of their desks, they would make some remark about her clothes, her hairstyle, or the way she walked. Once one of them blocked her way and rubbed up against her. Jane told him firmly that his behavior was not appreciated and she wished he would stop being so unpleasant. He just smiled and said, "Oh, come on. You love it."

Finally, Jane went to the supervisor to complain. He suggested that she was being too sensitive and should not let what was happening bother her. Still the harassment continued and Jane kept complaining to the supervisor. But now she started to keep a very accurate diary of the incidents. Each time one of her colleagues said or did something inappropriate she jotted it down. After a few months she placed the diary on the supervisor's desk with a memo making it very clear that she wanted action.

The supervisor decided to call the two consultants into his office. He demanded that both men apologize to Jane both verbally and in writing. As a result of his action the harassment stopped.

DEFINITION

Sexual harassment refers to any form of *unwanted* sexual attention on the job. It includes such conduct as sexual remarks, indecent suggestions, and offensive physical contact.

As many as three out of four reported cases involve supervisors who harass subordinates, such as an executive with a secretary or a foreman with a trainee. The rest occur when the victim of the harassment is a co-worker, client, patient, or student.

The Equal Employment Opportunity Commission (EEOC) issued this very complete definition in its 1980 guidelines on sexual harassment:

Unwelcome sexual advances, requests for sexual favors and other verbal or physical conduct of a sexual
nature constitute sexual harassment when:

(1) submission to such conduct is made either ex-
plicitly or implicitly a term or condition of an individual's employment,

(2) submission to or rejection of such conduct by
an individual is used as the basis for employment
decisions affecting such individual, or

(3) such conduct has the purpose or effect of unreasonably interfering with an individual's work performance or creating an intimidating, hostile, or offensive working environment.

INCIDENCE

On a nationwide basis the problem of sexual harassment is
known to be very great among working women. But exact
facts and figures on the extent of the problem are difficult
to come by. Most women hesitate to talk about incidents in
which they have been involved. Some are afraid of losing
their jobs. Others blame themselves for having provoked the
conduct in the first place.

Of the 48 million women in the work force an estimated
30 to 40 million, about seven out of every ten, will be sexually harassed at some time in their working lives, according to Working Women's Institute (WWI). The WWI is a non-
profit organization established in 1975 to address the issue
of sexual harassment. The Women's Legal Defense Fund also
put the incidence of sexual harassment at about 70 percent.

Ninety percent of the nine thousand working women
surveyed by *Redbook* magazine in 1976 said that they had
experienced sexual harassment on the job. And another
source, the Federal Merit Systems Protection Board, in a
1981 survey of federal government employees revealed that
42 percent of the women had reported being sexually harassed within the preceding two years.

Recent evidence shows that sexual harassment is found not only in the work place. In February 1980 *Time* magazine cited a study of college graduates. Twenty-five percent of women with degrees in psychology reported unwanted sexual contact with their professors. Other research showed that numbers of women at Harvard University experienced sexual harassment. Thirty-two percent of the tenured female professors, 49 percent of those without tenure, 41 percent of the female graduate students, and 34 percent of the undergraduate women reported being sexually harassed in some form by an authority figure at least once while they were at the university.

The *United Methodist Reporter* (March 14, 1980) told of thirty-five incidents of sexual harassment at a church seminary in Dallas. And in the military, two male soldiers had to stand trial in March 1980 after they were accused of making "insulting advances" to female soldiers.

Sexual harassment can be verbal or physical. The most frequent verbal forms of sexual harassment are comments about a woman's body, jokes about her sexual behavior, direct propositions, and job-related threats for refusing sexual activity. The physical forms of harassing behavior include patting or pinching, frequent brushing against or touching another person's body, and rape.

Research of the WWI shows some of the harmful effects of sexual harassment on working women. In the majority (over 60 percent) of the cases they know of where a woman was harassed by a superior, the woman either was forced to resign, was fired, or was demoted. Many women registering for unemployment compensation give sexual harassment as the reason they quit their jobs. Those who resist unwanted advances may get poor job evaluations, receive unfavorable assignments, be denied promotion, or even lose their jobs.

Thus, the fear of losing wages, benefits, or the job itself, makes it difficult for women to complain. The victims of sexual harassment who decide not to take action often stay on the job. They remain trapped in an undignified or unfriendly environment because they feel that they cannot afford to leave. In this way sexual harassment contributes to

"Now, Miss Johnson, whatever would a nice girl
like you be wanting with equal pay?"

the feminization of poverty and to keeping women in entry-level, low-paying jobs.

Sexual harassment is often worse for women who hold jobs that employ very few female workers. It is believed to be one of the reasons women hesitate to take high-paying jobs in the so-called men's fields.

Most victims of sexual harassment suffer stress and anxiety. The constant tension, it is said, may cause nervous conditions, ulcers, asthma, and weight loss. Of the women reporting sexual harassment to WWI 99 percent said they had experienced guilt and depression. Thirty-eight percent reported physical symptoms such as migraine headaches, stomachaches, and higher blood pressure. Forty-six percent said their work performance suffered due to an inability to concentrate and a loss of ambition.

In 1980 the Illinois Task Force on Sexual Harassment in the Workplace, together with Sangamon State University, did a very thorough study of sexual harassment. The conclusions were based on questionnaires sent to 4,859 women, ranging in age from eighteen to seventy, in various departments and agencies of the Illinois state government.

Just over 30 percent of the women surveyed related sex-related incidents on the job that had "made them feel humiliated or threatened." Fifty-two percent said they had been the target of off-color remarks and teasing. About 41 percent reported "suggestive looks" or leers with sexual overtones made by male co-workers. Another 26 percent told how they had been pressured to provide sexual favors. There were 25 percent who had been touched or grabbed in ways they found offensive. Twenty percent had received sexual propositions. And finally, 9 percent spoke of other forms of sexual attention. (The total is over 100 percent because several women described more than one type or form of sexual harassment.)

The same study revealed what happened when the women did not cooperate with the sexual harasser. Six percent of the women were refused promotions they expected; 14 percent said someone they knew had not advanced in her job due to sexual harassment. Three percent had been transferred against their wishes; 10 percent knew of others who had been forced to move to other positions. Three percent had been fired; 13 percent knew others who had likewise lost their jobs. Seven percent had quit a job because of sexual harassment; 24 percent knew others who resigned under pressure. And 6 percent asked for transfers as a result of sexual harassment; 10 percent spoke of others who took different jobs.

SEXUAL HARASSMENT
AND THE LAW

On a business trip a supervisor observed a female attorney dancing with a co-worker. The supervisor told her not to socialize with other members of the staff. He also complained that her clothes were too tight and brightly colored. Over the following months the same supervisor continued to criticize her and finally had her fired.

The attorney filed a sex discrimination suit against the company, *Bellissimo* v. *Westinghouse* (1984). The court found that the supervisor's sex-based dislike of the woman was so strong that it was able "to alter the conditions of employment and create an abusive situation." The attorney was awarded $28,000 in current salary and $94,000 in back wages.

The courts now recognize sexual harassment as an unlawful employment practice because it causes different treatment of workers based on sex. Its victims are usually, but not always, women. (It is less common for women to harass male workers.) Sexual harassment is a form of discrimination, and as such is prohibited by Title VII of the Civil Rights Act of 1964. Title VII prohibits employment discrimination on the basis of race, color, religion, national origin, or sex.

The EEOC is the enforcement agency for Title VII. The EEOC guidelines of 1980 prohibit sexual harassment of employees under that law. The guidelines state that an employer should take all necessary steps to prevent sexual harassment. This includes raising the subject in an affirmative way, expressing strong disapproval, developing appropriate penalties, informing employees of their right to raise the issue of harassment under Title VII, and developing methods to increase everyone's awareness of the problem.

It is important, of course, to be able to draw a line between sexual harassment and warm social relationships between men and women. The EEOC has said it will determine whether conduct constitutes sexual harassment by looking "at the record as a whole and at the totality of the circumstances, such as the nature of the sexual advances and the context in which the alleged incidents occurred. The determination of the legality of a particular action will be made from the facts, on a case by case basis."

LEGAL HISTORY

In *Barnes* v. *Costle* (1977) a federal court of appeals explained for the first time why sexual harassment is prohibited under Title VII. The case involved Paulette Barnes, a payroll clerk at the Environmental Protection Agency. Ms. Barnes claimed that her supervisor frequently made sexual remarks to her and promised certain advantages if she went out with him. The federal appeals court ruling held that her employer had violated Title VII. "Plaintiff [Ms. Barnes] became the target of her supervisor's sexual desire because she was a woman, and was asked to bow to his demands as the price for holding her job." It held the agency responsible for this discrimination.

The fact that sexual harassment "unreasonably interfere[s] with an individual's performance or create[s] an intimidating, hostile, or offensive workplace" can qualify as an unlawful employment practice under Title VII. The case of *Bundy* v. *Jackson* (1981) set the precedent. Bundy charged that she had not been promoted because she had rejected sexual advances from her supervisors. The court found that the refusal of the advances had nothing to do with her failure to be promoted and that Title VII did not apply. But the higher Court of Appeals reversed the ruling.

It found that sexual harassment is sexual discrimination with respect to "terms, conditions or privileges of employment." This ruling helped other women who have not been fired or denied a promotion due to sexual harassment but just made to feel uncomfortable at work.

The *Continental Can Company* v. *Minnesota* (1981) is another landmark case. This one involves an employer's responsibility for harassment by co-workers. Willie Ruth Hawkins, one of only two women working in a plant of the Continental Can Company, complained to her supervisor of derogatory sexual remarks, offensive propositions, and unwanted physical contact from male co-workers. The supervisor took no action. She complained again when the abuse involved being grabbed from behind. Officials of the company told her that she had "to expect that kind of behavior when working with men." They also told her that they could not guarantee her safety on the job. She refused to return to work and sued the company. The court held the company liable. It stated that the employer has a duty to act when he knows of sexual harassment.

Sexual harassment may give rise to legal action if harmful conduct is intended. In *Kyriazi* v. *Western Electric Company* (1979) the woman lodging the complaint was able to show that the company's actions adversely affected her employment situation. Cleo Kyriazi said that three male workers in her department had teased, tormented, and criticized her in an unkind manner. The court found that though Kyriazi's supervisors were aware of the harassment, they did nothing. It held that Kyriazi's co-workers and supervisor were guilty of having seriously interfered with her employment contract.

In other instances, such as *Rogers* v. *L'Enfant Plaza Hotel* (1981), invasion of privacy was at issue. Ms. Rogers, a restaurant manager, sued the hotel where she worked. Ms. Rogers had complained to higher management about long and frequent harassment by her supervisor, including phone calls to her home. The management did not take any action. The court found that the phone calls to her home were an invasion of her privacy and ruled in her favor.

STUDENTS AND THE LAW

Unfortunately, the EEOC guidelines do not prohibit sexual harassment of students, unless the students are also employees. In that case they are covered by the guidelines that cover all other employees. But students are protected from sexual harassment by another law, Title IX of the Education Amendments of 1972.

Title IX prohibits sex discrimination against students and employees in educational institutions receiving federal assistance. Until now the only Title IX ruling having to do with the sexual harassment of a student is the case of *Alexander* v. *Yale* (1980). It involved a Yale University student who claimed that her political science professor had offered her an *A* in exchange for certain sexual favors. The case went to trial because "academic advancement conditioned upon submission to sexual demands constitutes sex discrimination in education." This ruling was important because it set a precedent for considering sexual harassment a violation of Title IX.

The Office for Civil Rights (OCR) at the Department of Education is the enforcement agency for Title IX. It has not yet issued any firm guidelines about whether Title IX covers sexual harassment. But the close resemblance between Title VII and Title IX would seem to show that sexual harassment of students is a form of sex discrimination. Future cases will further test whether the law can be applied to sexual harassment.

As you recall, in the case of *Grove City College* v. *Bell* (1984) the Supreme Court ruled that Title IX applied only to specific school programs or activities receiving federal dollars. Students who are sexually harassed, therefore, may now have legal protection only if the harassment occurs in a program or activity where federal money is directly involved.

The law is still new in the area of sexual harassment. But some women have already won victories in cases where they have sued harassers in civil or criminal actions. Many state departments of labor now consider sexual harassment

an intolerable job condition. Some will grant unemployment insurance benefits to women who leave their jobs for
this reason. Sexual harassment, however, is often difficult
to prove. A woman must know what to do, where to turn,
and who to tell if she is to receive protection under the law.

GETTING ACTION

In spite of the numbers of women who are harassed, few
know how to handle their anger and feelings of helpless-
ness. The most common ways are to ignore the incidents or
hope that they will stop. They are also among the least effective. According to a 1975 survey taken by WWI, in 75 percent of the cases where women ignored sexual harassment
the problem continued or grew worse.

The best advice is take action—and the sooner the better.

- Make a written record of what happened right away,
  including a description of the incident, the date, any
  conversation, and your reactions.

- Object to the harasser whenever and wherever you
  can. Tell him clearly that his attention is unwanted
  and offensive.

- Get. others to help you. If you suspect that others
  have been similarly treated, talk to them.

- Write a letter to the harasser. The letter might con-
  sist of three parts: part 1 to tell the facts of what has
  happened; part 2 to describe your feelings, opin-
  ions, or thoughts about what happened; and part 3
  to make very clear that you want the behavior to stop.

- Write a letter to the harasser's supervisor stating your
  complaint and asking that the harassment be
  stopped.

Someone who is sexually harassed can contact the EEOC
for information and assistance in filing a sex discrimina-

tion complaint under Title VII. It is important to know that before a working woman can sue in court under Title VII she must file a complaint or charge with the EEOC. The charge must be filed in person or in a letter that tells what occurred and when it happened. The woman should be sure to provide enough information to back up the complaint. Written notes on what happened and when, and who was there, are very useful in showing a pattern of unfair treatment.

The enforcement process begins with a fact-finding conference. If no satisfactory settlement is reached, the EEOC investigates further to decide whether or not discrimination has ocurred. The investigation usually involves a review of all relevant records, such as records of grievance procedures relating to sexual harassment. If reasonable cause of discrimination is found, the commission attorneys review the case again and decide whether they should sue the employer. If they decide against going to court, they issue a right-to-sue letter so that the woman can sue on her own.

A victim of sexual harassment also can file a suit under a number of state laws. The state laws that apply are those that protect individuals against assault, battery, intentional infliction of emotional distress, or intentional interference with an employment contract.

Writing a letter, filing a formal grievance or complaint, or taking legal action all take a lot of courage. But women in greater numbers than ever before are responding to the problem of sexual harassment as they find themselves being denied jobs or advancement at work or being forced to drop classes or accept lower grades in school.

VI

FACING THE FUTURE

Despite today's many laws and court decisions, women are still subject to widespread discrimination in the labor force. Employed women still are concentrated in the lowest-paying, least-valued jobs. They still suffer inequitable treatment in Social Security, pension, and insurance benefits. They are still affected by unfair practices and regulations in education. And they are still victims of sexual harassment.

Current laws are not fully adequate. Statutes and court decisions have not proved able to provide all the protection that is needed.

Federal, state, and local antidiscrimination laws in effect today can be reversed at any time. Affirmative action, equal opportunity, and equal education laws can be repealed or weakened by decisions of politicians or legislators.

The results of a Harris poll conducted in 1983 reported that 63 percent of Americans favored passage of an Equal Rights Amendment; men and women supported the amendment about equally. Of those who opposed the idea, two-thirds believed it was important to strengthen women's rights in economic areas, but they did not like the idea of a constitutional amendment.

To achieve full economic equality many believe it is necessary to adopt an Equal Rights Amendment (ERA) to the United States Constitution. The amendment would go a long way toward putting women's rights on a very firm foundation. It would withstand the pressures, urges, turnabouts, and changes of policy makers. And most of all, it would guarantee today's hard-won rights for the working women of tomorrow.

The amendment has been introduced into every Congress since 1923. Until it is passed, women's advocates will be pushing for the passage of other legislation that has many of the provisions of the ERA.

PROVISIONS
OF THE ERA

The ERA is proposed as the twenty-seventh amendment to the United States Constitution. It reads as follows:

Section 1: Equality of rights under the law shall not be denied or abridged by the United States or by any State on account of sex.

Section 2: The Congress shall have the power to enforce, by appropriate legislation, the provisions of this article.

Section 3: This amendment shall take effect two years after the date of ratification.

The fundamental principle of the ERA is simply that the federal government and all state and local governments must treat both men and women as individual persons, not on the basis of their sex. The amendment applies only to government action, such as equal pay and legal rights. It does not have anything to do with private actions or social relationships.

As we said, the ERA was first introduced in Congress in 1923. Since then some have viewed the amendment as the best way of eliminating sex discrimination in the land. Just as the Fourteenth Amendment was passed to guarantee equal protection under the law for blacks, the ERA would establish constitutional equality of the sexes.

For an amendment to become part of the Constitution it has to be passed by both the House of Representatives and the Senate and approved by thirty-eight states within ten years. In 1982 the ERA missed adoption by the narrow margin of three states. Nevertheless, it has many supporters who are pledged to keep working for its passage.

Public opinion polls show countrywide support for the provisions of the ERA. Some seventeen states have already indicated a commitment to equal rights by passing their own state ERA laws. The experience of the state ERAs is being used to show that the ERA is an effective way of getting fair and equal treatment for men and women.

EQUAL PAY

The ERA will clearly prohibit sex-based wage discrimination. It will narrow or eliminate the wage gap between men and women workers in federal, state, and local government. The government employs more people than any single private-sector industry. Once the government equalizes wages, it is expected that employers in the private sector will do the same.

Four generations of one family are shown here at an ERA rally in Chicago in 1980. In the foreground is Pauline Levin, 83; behind her and from left to right: daughter-in-law Elaine Levin, 50; Elaine's daughter, Lisa Backman, 25; Elaine's stepdaughter, Nancy Noteman, 27; and Nancy Noteman's daughter, Nora, 2.

Some opponents argue that ERA will destroy the family; they say that a woman's place is in the home, and that the amendment will force mothers to find jobs, leaving their children in the care of others.

As we have shown, the overwhelming numbers of women who work do so to pay their bills. The ERA will ensure the right to equal pay for the millions of women who need to work for whatever the reason. Also, the ERA will not force anyone to take a job. Individuals will still decide for themselves who in the family works outside the home.

Some are afraid that the amendment will mean the elimination of all "protective" labor laws for women. Among these are laws that exclude women from certain occupations, provide maximum working hours per day or per week for women, restrict the weights women employees may lift, preclude employment within certain periods before and after the delivery of a child, and require special facilities for women.

Supporters of ERA say that these protective laws were once useful. But now they have outlived their usefulness. As a matter of fact, in some cases these laws make it difficult or impossible for qualified women to be considered for certain jobs, often higher paying. Also, some court decisions have ruled that so-called protective legislation discriminates against women. This means it is in conflict with Title VII of the Civil Rights Act of 1964.

Laws that truly help women, such as those requiring rest periods and other health and safety measures, including child care leave, will be extended to apply equally to men. And benefits that cannot be extended to men will be eliminated. The guiding principle will be the equal treatment of both sexes.

SOCIAL SECURITY, PENSIONS, AND INSURANCE

According to the U.S. Commission on Civil Rights, the ERA will erase sex-based distinctions that treat one sex or the other unfairly. In their words it "will provide a constitutional basis for urging recognition of the value of the homemaker's contribution to a marriage. Ratification will keep the pressure on Congress to adopt reform legislation to eliminate the Social Security system's inequitable treatment of women."

The ERA, or other laws with similar provisions, will prohibit discrimination in pensions and in all types of insurance, including life, auto, disability, and health. Men and women will be equal in terms of the right to purchase such policies. The availability of coverage, terms, conditions, rates, benefits, requirements, and methods of determining them will be the same for men and women. Unisex insurance, using factors fairer than sex as a basis for deciding rates, will benefit everyone.

In the debate over the ERA some people say that women will lose their present Social Security benefits, which are based on their husbands' earnings. But this argument does not take into account the many factors that make present Social Security coverage out of date. The system ignores the economic value of a woman's work as homemaker. It fails to recognize that the modern American family no longer consists of one breadwinner and his dependents. And it does not consider the need of dependents for the same income security as the so-called breadwinner.

DISCRIMINATION IN EDUCATION AND SEXUAL HARASSMENT

The goal of the ERA is to put an end to sex discrimination in all publicly supported education programs. The amendment will direct the courts, as a matter of law, to correct any inequities based on sex in these educational institutions.

A number of critics of ERA say that the amendment will require men and women to share bathrooms, showers, locker rooms, and dormitory rooms in schools. The history of the state ERAs, though, makes it very clear that the ERA will definitely not require such sharing. The constitutional right to privacy will still justify separate facilities for men and women.

Throughout the country court decisions and laws growing out of state ERAs have extended the legal rights of both women and men in education. In Massachusetts, for example, female law students won the right to apply for scholarships previously awarded only to male students. And girls in Philadelphia recently were given permission, for the first time, to enter the prestigious, previously all-male Central High School. A federal ERA would make such practices the law of the land.

Under the ERA women also will obtain equal treatment in the military. This will correct discrimination that currently denies women many educational opportunities in the armed services. Since the military is often exempted from the provisions of the current antidiscrimination laws, there have been some abuses. Women in the armed forces often find themselves concentrated in the traditionally female job categories and subject to sexual harassment. The amendment will require the government to assign men and women jobs based on their individual skills and abilities, not on old, fixed ideas of their roles and abilities.

The ERA will not require that all women serve in the military. The history of the amendment makes clear that women will be subject to a draft, if we have one, just as men are. But Congress could exempt mothers just as it did fathers in the most recent drafts. A Senate ERA report reads as follows: "Thus the fear that mothers will be conscripted from their children into military service if the Equal Rights Amendment is ratified is totally and completely unfounded. Congress will retain ample power to create legitimate sex-neutral exemptions from compulsory services. For example, Congress might well exempt all parents of children under eighteen from the draft."

The ERA also will bolster the EEOC guidelines. The guidelines, you remember, call for strong measures to eliminate sexual harassment in the federal government. It will improve the ways people may register complaints and better the kinds of help available to victims.

SUMMARY

Antidiscrimination laws and state ERAs have expanded employment and educational opportunities for both men and women. But there are still many problems to be solved and many wrongs to be righted. Based on its study of the ERA the U.S. Commission on Civil Rights urged ratification of the amendment to achieve equal rights for women and men. "The women and men of this country," they said, "deserve no less than this secure, constitutional guarantee of equal dignity under the law."

Brown, Barbara A. et al. *Women's Rights and the Law.* New York: Praeger, 1977.

Cassedy, Ellen, and Nussbaum, Karen. *Nine to Five: The Working Woman's Guide to Office Survival.* New York: Penguin, 1983.

Coalition on Women and the Budget. *The Inequality of Sacrifice: The Impact of the Reagan Budget on Women.* Washington, 1984.

Dzeich, Billie Wright, and Weiner, Linda. *The Lecherous Professor.* Boston: Beacon Press, 1984.

Howe, Louise Kapp. *Pink Collar Workers.* New York: Putnam, 1977.

Kahn-Hut, Rachel, and Daniels, Arlene K. *Women and Work.* New York: Oxford University Press, 1982.

Kessler-Harris, Alice. *Out to Work: A History of Wage-Earning Women in the United States.* New York: Oxford University Press, 1982.

————. *Women Have Always Worked: A Historical Overview.* New York: The Feminist Press and McGraw-Hill, 1981.

Kreps, Juanita. *Sex in the Marketplace: American Women at Work.* Baltimore: Johns Hopkins Press, 1971.

League of Women Voters Education Fund. *Achieving Sex Equity in Vocational Education: A Crack in the Wall.* Publication No. 493. Washington, 1982.

National Commission on Working Women. *National Survey of Working Women.* Washington, 1979.

National Committee on Pay Equity. *The Wage Gap: Myths and Facts.* Washington, 1980.

————. *Equal Pay for Work of Comparable Value.* Washington, 1980.

National Science Foundation. *Women and Minorities in Science and Engineering.* Washington, 1984.

National Women's Law Center. *Sex Discrimination in Education: Legal Rights and Remedies.* Washington, 1984.

Nine to Five. *The 9 to 5 National Survey on Women and Stress.* Cleveland: Nine to Five, 1983.

Project on the Status and Education of Women. *Classroom Climate*. Washington, 1982.

————. *Rape and Sexual Harassment*. Washington, 1978.

Ross, Susan Deller, and Barcher, Ann. *The Rights of Women*. New York: Bantam, 1983.

Smith, Ralph. *The Subtle Revolution*. Washington: Urban Institute, 1979.

Stromberg, Ann, and Harkness, Shirley. *Women Working*. Palo Alto, Calif.: Mayfield, 1978.

Terkel, Studs. *Working*. New York: Pantheon, 1974.

United States Department of Labor, Woman's Bureau. *Time of Change: 1983 Handbook on Women Workers*. Washington: Government Printing Office, 1983.

————. *A Woman's Guide to Apprenticeship*. Pamphlet 17. Washington: Government Printing Office, 1980.

————. *A Working Woman's Guide to Her Job Rights*. Washington: Government Printing Office, 1980.

————. *Regulations to Help Open Nontraditional Jobs to Women*. Washington: Government Printing Office, 1980.

————. *State Labor Laws in Transition: From Protection to Equal Status for Women*. Washington: Government Printing Office, 1980.

Waite, Linda. *U.S. Women at Work*. Santa Monica, Calif.: Rand, 1981.

Women's Equity Alliance League. *Economic Agenda for 1984*. Washington, 1983.

Women's Legal Defense Fund. *Employment Discrimination Laws: A Handbook*. Washington, 1980.

————. *Legal Remedies for Sexual Harassment*. Washington, 1983.

Women's Research and Education Institute of the Congresswomen's Caucus. *Older Women: The Economics of Aging*. Washington, 1980.

————. *Working and Women in the 1980s: A Perspective on Basic Trends Affecting Women's Jobs and Job Opportunities*. Washington, 1983.

Center for Women Policy Studies
2000 P Street, NW
Suite 508
Washington, DC 20036
(202) 872-1770

Coalition of Labor Union Women
386 Park Avenue South
New York, NY 10016
(212) 679-0765

Congressional Caucus
    for Women's Issues
2471 Rayburn Building
Washington, DC 20515
(202) 225-6740

Department of Labor
Office of Federal Contract
    Compliance Programs
200 Constitution Avenue, NW
Washington, DC 20010

Department of Labor
Office of the Secretary
Women's Bureau
Washington, DC 20210
(202) 523-6611

Eagle Forum
Alton, IL 62002
(618) 462-5415

Equal Employment Opportunity
    Commission (EEOC)
2401 E Street, NW
Washington, DC 20506
(202) 655-4000

Federally Employed Women (FEW)
National Press Building, Room 481
Washington, DC 20045
(202) 638-4404

League of Women Voters
1730 M Street, NW
Washington, DC 20036
(202) 429-1965

Legal Defense and Educational Fund (NOW/LDEF)
99 Hudson Street
New York, NY 10013
(212) 828-4420

National Commission on Working Women
2000 P Street, NW, Suite 508
Washington, DC 20036
(202) 872-1782

National Committee on Pay Equity
c/o National Education Association
1202 Sixteenth Street, NW
Room 615
Washington, DC 20036
(202) 833-4324

National Council on the Future
    of Women in the Workplace
2012 Massachusetts Avenue, NW
Washington, DC 20036
(202) 293-1100

National Federation of Business
    and Professional Women's Clubs
2012 Massachusetts Avenue, NW
Washington, DC 20036
(202) 293-1100

National Organization for Women (NOW)
425 Thirteenth Street, NW
Washington, DC 20004
(202) 347-2279

National Women's Law Center
1751 N Street, NW
Washington, DC 20036
(202) 872-0670

National Women's Political Caucus
1411 K Street, NW
Room 1110
Washington, DC 20005
(202) 347-4456

9 to 5
National Association of Working Women
1313 L Street, N.W.
Washington, DC 20005
(202) 898-3200

Pension Rights Center
1346 Connecticut Avenue, NW
Washington, DC 20036
(202) 296-3778

Project on Equal Educational
    Rights (NOW/PEER)
1413 K Street, NW
Washington, DC 20005
(202) 332-7337

Project on the Status and Education
    of Women
Association of American Colleges
1818 R Street, NW
Washington, DC 20009

Stop Sexual Abuse of Students
c/o Chicago Public Education Project
American Friends Service Committee
407 S. Dearborn Street
Chicago, IL 60605

Women's Equity Action League (WEAL)
805 Fifteenth Street, NW
Suite 822
Washington, DC 20005
(202) 638-1961

Women's Legal Defense Fund
2000 P Street, NW
Suite 400
Washington, DC 20036
(202) 887-0364

Women's Research and Education Institute
204 Fourth Street, SE
Washington, DC 20003
(202) 546-1010

Women's Rights Project
American Civil Liberties Union
132 West 43rd Street
New York, NY 10036
(212) 944-9800

Working Women's Institute (WWI)
593 Park Avenue
New York, NY 10021
(212) 828-4420